THE SILENCED ARMY

THE SILENCED ARMY

nichole chavez

Raquel,
No longer silenced!
Nichole

EQUIP PRESS

Colorado Springs

Published by Equip Press, Colorado Springs, CO

First Edition: 2019
The Silenced Army / Nichole Chavez
Paperback ISBN: 978-1-946453-87-7
eBook ISBN: 978-1-946453-88-4

A NOTE FROM NICHOLE

I BELIEVE WE, the Christian women of the world, are at a crossroads. We can choose to remain silent while the world cries out for the message of Jesus, or we can stand up and volunteer to bring the Savior into our world.

For far too long we have stayed silent–we have allowed the pressures of sin and this world to distract us and silence us from stepping into our purpose and calling. The world's message is strong; it is unified and it has momentum. We have allowed our voice to fade into silence, and we have been stuck in our pain and hurt for far too long. We have been a silenced army. But that is about to change!

In sharing my hurt, pain, and experiences, it is my prayer that you will be encouraged, motivated, and inspired to stand when the world says bow, use your voice when you feel pressured to stay silent, and embrace your purpose and calling. Let's change the world for Jesus.

—***Nichole***

TO MY HUSBAND, JAMES,

Thank you for loving me unconditionally, encouraging me,
pushing me, inspiring me, and leading me.
You have encouraged me to use my voice in the silence, stand when others kneel, and silence the voice of doubt, discouragement, insecurity, and unworthiness.
You have stood up for me and with me when you were pressured not to.
You have led me to not only step into my purpose and calling but to do so boldly, unapologetically, courageously, and humbly.
Thank you for encouraging me to live the life God has called me to live so I can stand before him at the end of my life having completed all he had planned for me.

TO MY SON, KYLE,

Thank you for always stopping what you are doing to help me work out phrasing and wording.
Your contributions to this book will forever be in print and will leave a lasting mark on this world. Thank you for picking your sister up from school, taking Zander to the vet, and grocery shopping for me while I was writing this book. Thank you for being you—
loving, supportive, and helpful—
and for the unsolicited shoulder rubs after a long day of writing.

TO MY DAUGHTER, NICHELLE,

You have inspired courage in me, and your life has brought healing into the broken parts of mine. You unknowingly are a hero to our family and so many others with the testimony that is your life.
Your words, "I am so proud of you momma," fuel me, encourage me, and remind me of the legacy I am leaving. Thank you for freely, effortlessly, and frequently showering me with words of encouragement and love.

I know God stands with us and says,
"Now this is a family I can change the world through."

CONTENTS

A Note from Nichole 5

1. The Silenced Army 11
2. Silenced By Fear 21
3. Silenced By Pain 31
4. Silenced By Doubt 43
5. Silenced By Unforgiveness 53
6. Silenced By Shame 65
7. Silenced By Offense 77
8. Silenced By Pride 87
9. Silenced By Culture 99
10. Silenced By Distraction 111
11. The Army 123

1 THE SILENCED ARMY

Years ago, I read a post on social media that said, "My 6-year-old daughter came home from church today saying 'I want to be a pastor and preach about Jesus.'" The mom replied to the daughter, "Girls are not preachers, but you can work in the nursery."

The silenced army. Generation after generation silenced. Purpose and calling wasted by the advice and words of well-intentioned people, with unintentional consequences.

Women–the silenced army of God. Created on purpose and with a purpose. Created to change the world around us for Jesus.

We were created, resilient, strong, caring, compassionate, loving, hopeful, courageous, skilled, intelligent, creative, brave, and passionate, just to name a few.

We are risk takers, heart menders, advice givers, faith builders, and history makers.

We are also broken, stubborn, prideful, selfish, fearful, doubtful, jealous, and sinful.

Not one of us are all these things, but each of us are some of these things. We push each other to strength or push each other to silence.

Together we are an army. We are a volunteer army. We are women created by God on purpose and for a purpose. We were created to change the world around us for Jesus.

Silenced by fear, pain, doubt, unforgiveness, shame, offense, pride, culture, and distraction. Half of God's army is being attacked with these conquerable battles, but instead of fighting, we stand silenced, unaware that the battle being fought requires all of us to make a stand using our purpose, calling, actions, and voice to bring Jesus into our world again.

We live in a time where women are no longer afraid to stand up for their beliefs, fight for the right to choose their own path, and make choices for their own benefit.

Women are making progress. They are changing the world; they are making a difference.

We now have the right to kill babies in the womb, we have the right to celebrate abortion and encourage the next generation of women to make a choice for life or death for the human being they carry. We are now allowed to view every pregnancy after conception as a choice.

We are making progress. We are changing the world. We are making a difference.

We have the right and mandate to stay silent in every school across America about our relationship with Jesus and our Christ-centered beliefs. We can no longer pray or talk about Jesus. We can no longer share the hope and healing we have found in Jesus with a generation that is killing themselves over bullying, depression, loneliness, anxiety, and rejection. Our kids have been led to believe it's against the law to bring a Bible to school or pray at school, at least that is what my daughter was told by other students.

We now have the right to marry whomever we want and be whatever gender we want to be. We have the right to throw God's workmanship and masterpiece out the window, because we believe that we know better than him. We have the right to blackball, blacklist, and protest anyone who doesn't condone the right to oppose God.

The world is telling us we are making progress. We are changing the world. We are making a difference. And the world is right.

We shape the world with the sound of our voice or with the lack of our voice. We cast our vote when we stay silent; we give our approval with the lack of action. We are changing the world by remaining silent; we are making a difference by not making one at all.

We, the Christian women of this world, are a silenced army. Silenced by the voice in our head, silenced by the pressures of this world, silenced by each other, silenced by the doubt that we can make a difference, silenced by our lack of trust in God, and silenced by the ever-present voice of the enemy.

We are a volunteer army. We volunteered to be changed by Jesus so we can change the world for Jesus. We don't have to become victims of this sinful world, but rather volunteers to change it.

Volunteers to change the world for Jesus.
Volunteers to speak truth to the lies of the world.
Volunteers to bring hope to the hopeless.
Volunteers to protect the unborn.
Volunteers to give voice to the unseen, overlooked, and undervalued.
Volunteers to step into the purpose God created you to fulfill.
Volunteers to stay silent when all we have to contribute to hate is fuel.
Volunteers to protect marriage between a man and a woman.
Volunteers to not be offended by ignorance.
Volunteers to bring healing to a divided world.

In Genesis, we read about the creation of the world. In six days, God created everything we see and don't see. He created a masterpiece and called it good. He created man in his image; he created us in his image. God, in his infinite wisdom, created the perfect world and universe, complete and missing nothing. But wait, where is the woman? Did he forget about her? No, he saved the final piece that completed his masterpiece for last.

I love to put together puzzles, and the most satisfying piece to place is the last one. That last piece completes the picture—the last piece makes it whole, makes it perfect. Eve was the final piece in God's perfect puzzle. God put her in place as the completing piece, the piece that makes everything whole. God doesn't forget anything. Eve wasn't an afterthought; she was the finishing touch.

We are the final puzzle piece; we are a crucial piece in his plan. We were created on purpose and with a purpose. We were created to change the world for Jesus.

We are not the only ones who know that we can change the world for Jesus—Satan knows as well. He knows we were created on purpose and with a purpose, and he knows what that purpose is. We are a threat; we are his enemy.

Satan targeted Eve because she was the missing piece in his plan. She was the piece he needed to bring sin into our world. He needed Eve to bring shame to an entire gender—he needed her to start the silenced army. An army reminded of sin and shamed because of it. The ashamed army is an ineffective army, an immobile army, a scattered army—it is a silenced army.

A silenced army allows battles to be won without a fight; it will enable them to be surrounded and made to comply. A silenced army can only sit around and complain to an empty room about the battles being lost, the ground that's been taken, and the treasures that have been stolen.

A silenced army becomes victims of the world rather than volunteers to change it.

Although silenced (for now), we are an army. We are an army united by God. We are an army with the common goal of sharing Jesus with the world, who wants the next generation to carry the message of Jesus forward, and an army that wants to stop and drown out the voice of the enemy with the message and righteousness of Jesus. We are an army motivated by love, emboldened by our faith, and equipped by our God.

We have to accept that we can make a difference, even though the enemy is counting on us not figuring this out. He wants to keep us divided and separated from each other; he wants us to feel alone in our Christ-centered beliefs and to feel defeated and overwhelmed. He wants us to carry fear, pain, doubt, unforgiveness, shame, offense, lies, and pride so we will never come together as one voice and one army. The enemy wants us to retreat, cower, and bow to culture, distraction, and fear.

Scattered as we are, we are an army that can change the world for Jesus.

"For where two or three gather in my name, there am I with them."

MATTHEW 18:20 NIV

We are more than two or three, we are millions. Romans 8:31 NIV says,

"What, then, shall we say in response to these things? If God is for us, who can be against us?"

The luxury of sitting back and letting others fight the battle is over. We are running out of time—the mission is critical and the electricity in the air is urgency. As I write this, my heart is pounding, because I know these words to be true. If ever there was a time for all of us to unite, it is now. I can see the enemy closing in—he is aggressive in his agenda to steal and kill and destroy, without hesitation or discrimination. We as a collective whole, and as individuals, are all targets.

"The thief's purpose is to steal and kill and destroy."

JOHN 10:10a NLT

He is living out his purpose to the fullest; his plan is in full motion and picking up steam. We have to get ahead of him if we want to make a difference. We have to speak up and speak out; we have to act on the purpose God has put inside of each of us if we want to change the world for Jesus.

The enemy is stealing, killing, and destroying our babies, young people, family units, marriages, relationships, and the list goes on. The battle is real, and it needs you in it. Every single one of us has a God-given, unique-to-us purpose, that purpose is necessary in the army.

Every single one of us matters, every purpose realized and accomplished, every one of us marching in unison.

"The human body has many parts,
but the many parts make up one whole body.
So it is with the body of Christ."
1 CORINTHIANS 12:12 NLT

Let me make something clear. Satan is not stealing, killing, and destroying our way of life—our morals, our preferences, or tolerances. He is stealing, killing, and destroying God's way of life. The life God set in motion—the morals he put in place, the guardrails he set up, and the laws he put in place. When we accept Jesus and volunteer for the army of Christ, we agree to fight for and uphold the message of Jesus, not our own.

We don't get to interpret the Bible as we see fit, and we don't get to pick and choose which parts we will follow and which ones we won't. We can't be pressured by society to accept things as right that God says are wrong. We don't get to contradict God. We don't get to define sin. We get to fight with him and for him.

Our weapons are not meant to destroy people, but to bring life to them. The message of Jesus will replace lies with truth, bring hope to the hopeless, healing to the sick and broken, joy to the depressed, peace to the anxious, direction to the lost, significance to the unseen, freedom to the enslaved, a hearing ear to the unheard, and Heaven to the hellbound.

We can't be afraid or ashamed to bring these rare and precious gifts to a world that so badly needs them. We are the front line of hope, the face of healing, and the voice of God.

At 14 years old, I decided I would more than likely attend church when I was a "grown-up," but I made up my mind that I would never date or marry a pastor. At the time, I was a pastor's daughter. I hated every single moment of it, and I wasn't shy about voicing it. My mom could probably show you some strongly-worded letters I used to write on this very topic. I would unapologetically say, "My parents were called to ministry, not me, so why do I have to suffer." This idea was so rooted within me that when my husband (who was a pastor's son) asked me to marry him, I said, "Yes, as long as you promise to never work for a church." He promised he wouldn't, we shook hands on it, and I said yes to his proposal. It's funny now, because my husband has been a pastor for the past 15 years, but at that time it was no laughing matter. I took one of the most important and special times of my life to secure my future: a future without full-time service to God, his church, and his people.

Looking back, I am shocked at how short-sighted I was. I never thought I had to worry about my purpose and calling, and I never thought I would one day have the title and calling of pastor. Never once did I think I would write books and studies that would encourage women all around the world to accept that they have a purpose, and then teach them how to step into it so, together, we can change the world for Jesus. Never did I think I would start a ministry that encourages women to see themselves as world changers–not as victims of this sinful world, but as volunteers to change it.

I was so busy making sure my husband, James, didn't become a pastor that I totally missed what God had for me. I can now see that the enemy had me exactly where he wanted me. He had me so distracted and focused on controlling my *husband's* future that I couldn't see that God had a purpose for *mine*.

The enemy knew if he could keep me silent, he would silence my husband and my kids. Through me, he could have silenced everyone that is encouraged to speak out, step up, and step into their purpose through the message God has given me to share. He knew the consequences of my silence would go far beyond me–it would impact generations to come. Just like Eve's sin changed the world forever, so does our purpose, sin, and silence. It is time for us to own the consequences of our silence, repent, then stand up to the enemy. Let's use our God-given purpose to change the world for Jesus.

He only has to silence one of us to silence the rest, for if one of us speaks up, it gives courage to the rest.

I am one voice of many (but still too few) that are speaking up and asking you to join the movement against fear, pain, doubt, unforgiveness, shame, offense, pride, culture, and distraction that has silenced this army. We have been silenced for too long–together let's find our purpose, calling, voice, and actions and use them to silence the enemy. Together, let's stand up for the lost, broken, hurt, abused, forgotten, unseen, enslaved, and overlooked.

"This is my command—be strong and courageous!
Do not be afraid or discouraged.
For the LORD your God is with you wherever you go."
JOSHUA 1:9 NLT

We aren't expected to have all the answers on how to change the world for Jesus, but we are expected to seek out the answers. We are expected to bring to light what is in the shadows that silences us and then have the courage to face them. We have sat back and watched the battle from a distance for far too long. It is time to get into the fight; it's time to no longer be a silenced army but a mobilized, effective, strong, courageous, and united army so we can change the world for Jesus.

This book is for all the volunteers who want to see your life, your world, and our world changed for Jesus. There will be no victims on this journey, no feeling sorry for ourselves, and no wondering why God chose us. Instead, we will be excited that God chose us and together, we as an army of volunteers, will change the world for Jesus.

2 SILENCED BY FEAR

The home phone rings. My mom answers, then hands me the phone and says, "It's your dad, he wants to talk to you." Confused, I say, "Hello." He proceeds to tell me that he will be home late and wouldn't be home for dinner. I said, "ok," with the tone only a teenage girl who is confused can have. We hung up, and my heart sank. I knew something was wrong. I went up to my bedroom and dialed *69. For those of you who were born after the age of the dinosaurs and don't know what that specific number combination does, I'll tell you. When you dial *69, a recording will read back the number that the last call came from. I quickly wrote the number down, then slowly dialed it. Two rings later, a woman answered the phone, and I knew why he wasn't coming home.

My dad was bi-vocational. His professions were police officer and pastor. He was sworn to uphold the law of the land and the laws of God—he was supposed to be immune to sin like this; in my mind he was supposed to be better than this.

My heart hurt at the betrayal of it all, and my heart ached because my mom didn't know yet and someone had to tell her. I knew that life would never be the same, and the uncertainty of my future made me sick to my stomach.

I so badly wanted to forget what I knew. I wanted the burden of knowing this information to be shared, so I called my older brother. After a sibling meeting with both of my brothers, we decided to confront my dad with what we knew to be true.

I thought it would be hard to confront him, but the hardest part was being lied to. He held his ground and denied it all. By this time, we had more evidence; we knew the truth, but he wasn't willing to admit to it. He laughed at us, told us we were just kids and we didn't know what we were talking about, he told us to mind our own business, and then he kicked us out of his church office. If only this were the first time he had mocked us or lied to us, but sadly we were used to seeing the man behind the pulpit and the man at home as two different people.

My mom found out about the affair within a few weeks of that meeting and, as expected, our whole world fell apart. The man we saw at home was the man they finally saw at church. It was oddly comforting and terrifying at the same time. After many attempts by the elders of our church to walk my dad through the process of repentance and healing–without much success–my dad was asked to step down. We quietly left the church that my parents started in our living room, the one I hated so much, the one my parents sacrificed time with us for, and the one that I swore I would never be a part of when I was a "grown-up." We left and my heart was broken.

After leaving the church, I felt empty, ashamed, hurt, and afraid. I decided the church did this to my family, and God allowed this to happen. I decided this will not be my life, this will not be my story, this will not be my outcome. I will not marry a pastor, and I will not entrust my life, heart, future, and family to people–and without knowing it, I had decided that I didn't trust God either.

Even though I hadn't done anything wrong, I felt the shame of my father's sins. I hid from the people who knew the details. I ran from anything or anyone that reminded me of the pain. I ran from God with the vow that this would never happen when I had a family of my own. God and the church would not wreck my life. I thought following God had painful consequences and I feared it. I feared God and any plans he had for me.

Fear silenced me.

Fear will silence an army.

We, the Christian women of this world, are a silenced army. Silenced by fear. The enemy has used fear to silence our army since the beginning of time. He uses our experiences—both past and present—to stop us from showing up and speaking up. He tells us standing up for what God says is right will bring a firestorm of controversy, rejection, hurt, embarrassment, abandonment, isolation, and persecution. He tells us that if we give in to God and step into our purpose that we will be asked to do things out of our comfort zone, go places out of the safe zone, or put ourselves in the danger zone.

The Bible is full of stories about people who were put in impossible positions where they are forced to wait on God to save them, forced to make a decision for Christ before they know the outcome, or forced to stand—even if they stand alone.

Even if they stand alone.

Shadrach, Meshach, and Abednego are the perfect examples of this scenario. This story can be found in Daniel chapter three.

King Nebuchadnezzar decreed that everyone in his kingdom must bow down to the gold statue made in his image. If they didn't, they would be thrown into a fiery furnace and be burned to death. When the music sounded, everyone bowed except three men: Shadrach, Meshach, and Abednego. They wouldn't bend their knees to the idol, because they only bowed to God. I am sure they weren't the only three people who knew they shouldn't bow to the statue, but every person there bowed anyway out of fear. Their life was more important to them than standing out, standing up, and standing firm.

Fear silenced an army of people and brought them to a bow. Fear left only three people standing. Only three people decided that they would not be a part of the silenced army.

We respond to fear three different ways:

1. We run from it.
2. We run to a solution.
3. We bow to it.

I bowed to the pressure of fear. I vowed to oppose God and his plan for my life in exchange for the safety of an ordinary life–a life of fighting my purpose and fighting God–fearing one day I might give in and it might cost me everything. That's the real fear we all face. We think that if we give in to God and choose his way, his plan, and his path, we might lose everything we see as important. I certainly bought into that lie. I bowed.

Shadrach, Meshach, and Abednego knew their decision to stand and not bow down to the statue would cost them their lives; yet they chose to run to the solution which was God. We tell ourselves that there are acceptable reasons for giving in to fear: God will understand that we are trying to preserve our way of life, God doesn't want me to be uncomfortable, or I don't want to get hurt. I believed these lies, and I clung to them as my reasonable excuse. I had been hurt; I watched the hypocritical life of my dad as he destroyed our family and shook the faith of so many other people. I had a reasonable excuse. Shadrach, Meshach, and Abednego knew that fear was not an excuse for their bowing, and they refused to be silenced because they knew God.

"Shadrach, Meshach, and Abednego replied, 'O Nebuchadnezzar, we do not need to defend ourselves before you. If we are thrown into the blazing furnace, the God whom we serve is able to save us. He will rescue us from your power, Your Majesty. But even if he doesn't, we want to make it clear to you, Your Majesty, that we

will never serve your gods or worship the gold statue you have set up.'"

DANIEL 3:16-18 NLT

Shadrach, Meshach, and Abednego start out by saying, "We do not need to defend ourselves before you." What a clear way to start their conversation with King Nebuchadnezzar. We have lost that kind of courage. We feel the need to water down God's truths for fear of offending someone, and we stay silent for fear of being seen as intolerant. These three men didn't feel a need to defend their obedience to God or their devotion to him. They knew their "why" and were unwilling to debate it.

God's truths are not debatable!

"The God whom we serve is able to save us." They knew what God can do; they knew his power is infinite and has no limitations. Their intimate knowledge of God gave them the confidence, peace, and courage to not bow down to fear.

"He will rescue us from your power." They showed faith and trust that God would rescue them, while at the same time acknowledging that King Nebuchadnezzar had power. We know our enemy has power; he can bring fear into our lives as a distraction from the faith we should have in God. Our confidence and our solution to fear is to know who God is and to know without a hint of fear that he can and will rescue us.

They finish with the incredible response to fear: "But even if he doesn't, we want to make it clear to you, Your Majesty, that we will never serve your gods or worship the gold statue you have set up."

"But even if he doesn't" is where we usually get stuck. We don't want the clause "but even if he doesn't," we want the reassurance of the verses above, the "he will" and "he can" clause. We want the assurance that if we stand up to fear—if we leave the safety of the silenced army—that we will be protected and rescued. Fear silenced is what gives us the faith and confidence to say, "but even if he doesn't." That had to be a sweet, peaceful place to be in their hearts. No fear: just them and God standing in the midst of a bowing world.

There is safety in numbers; the silenced army is vast, and you will never be singled out or made to stand alone. You will never be called upon to do something out of the ordinary or be forced to stand when the rest of the world bows. You will never be asked to do anything except stay silent.

The army silenced by fear will never do anything at all.

It will watch as the world turns against God. It will observe the destruction of human life and close its eyes and ears to suffering. It will bow when it's supposed to stand.

The army that doesn't know that God can and will rescue them is a silenced army.

The army of three that was Shadrach, Meshach, and Abednego did get thrown into the fiery furnace. A furnace so hot that it killed the guards who threw them into it. Their faith carried them through the ridicule and through the flames.

When we stand up and leave the silenced army, we do it with all the faith we can muster up; we do it knowing we may be the only one standing, the only one speaking out, and the only one willing to go through the fire.

Something amazing and special happens when you think you are going to be standing alone, but are willing to do it anyway. That is when the silenced army becomes *The Army*: When Jesus steps into the fire with you and you realize you were never alone. You see for the first time that the battle is not over–it needs you and the purpose God created you to live out. That is when you see God.

Daniel 3:24-25 NLT tells us the rest of the story.

> *"But suddenly, Nebuchadnezzar jumped up in amazement and exclaimed to his advisers, 'Didn't we tie up three men and throw them into the furnace?' 'Yes, Your Majesty, we certainly did,' they replied. 'Look!' Nebuchadnezzar shouted. 'I see four men,*

unbound, walking around in the fire unharmed! And the fourth looks like a god!'"

When you silence fear and stand for your faith, people won't see you standing there alone; they will see Jesus too. They may not agree with you or with Jesus, but they will see him. They will know that he never lets us walk through the fire alone. He never leaves us or forsakes us, and he will never abandon us.

We will never stand alone. The silenced army may seem safe and may feel comfortable, but it is an illusion. The fighting is happening, and the losing army isn't just going home in defeat: It is annihilated. Our opponent is out to kill, steal, and destroy. He is out for the eternity of everyone on this planet and for the souls of the people you love.

It's time to stand; it's time to become *The Army*.

James and I got married, and I was happy. I finally had the peace and unconditional love I had always wanted. James is calm, cool, and collected; he is patient, supportive, loving and made just for me. I didn't know that kind of love was possible, yet there I was with the most precious gift a girl could ask for.

I was so happy that I was miserable. I was so afraid that one day I could lose it all, and in my fearful mind, if he ever worked for a church it was almost a guarantee. My fear pushed me to protect my little family with everything in me. To stand guard even against God.

James and I found a church to attend that we both loved. We were growing spiritually, and I was learning to trust God a little bit more each day. That trust was tested when James got a call from the pastor one afternoon. I remember like it was yesterday. We were sitting at the kitchen table talking when his phone rang. He answered it and it was our pastor. Sitting next to James, I could hear every word. He said, "James have you ever thought about going into full-time ministry?" My heart dropped into my stomach and I could barely breathe. My immediate response was to look James straight in the eye and emphatically shake my head no. The look in my eyes was a mixture of a warning and a threat–and completely terrified. With my eyes, I was trying to remind James that he promised he would never work for a church, and based on his reaction, I think he got the message.

This was the moment I tried so hard to avoid, the conversation I feared most. This was my worst nightmare come true.

James' response put me at ease. He said, "No, but thank you." A few weeks later, the phone rings, and it's our pastor, again. He tells James, "I really feel led to ask you again, would you be willing to come into the office? We can have a conversation and I can answer questions you may have." James said he would and asked if I could join them for the conversation. James knew that I would not like it if I didn't have a chance to hear what this pastor (who was trying to ruin my life) had to say.

At this point fear is raging. I was in full-on panic mode. I thought I knew pastors; I thought they were all the same and just like my dad. Pastors cheat, they are mean and abusive, and they don't live what they teach–in short, they are humans and can't be trusted.

We drove together to the meeting, sat in the pastor's office, and with shaking hands and a thumping heart, I listened to our pastor's heart for the church and the ministry they wanted to hire James to be involved in. Even though I didn't want to, I started to get excited: my fear was waning, and my heart was softening. This only increased my anxiety and panic. The words, "No, Nichole, this is not what you want, this could destroy everything you have," were screaming in my mind the whole time. Fear had a grip on me and was not about to let go.

James and I drove home, talking the whole way, rehashing the entire conversation and picking apart every word for hidden meanings and expectations. We listed the pros and cons extensively, leaving no imaginary outcome off of the list. I harbored each and every con as a possible reality in my mind. It was exhausting! I was tired of fighting God; I was tired of protecting my life. I listened to the excitement in James' voice and badly wanted him to be happy. I wanted him to accept this job but at the same time, I really, really, didn't.

That night I did something I had never done before. I stopped running from God, and I ran *to* God. I cried my eyes out, bared my soul, shared every fear, and laid my broken and fearful heart out for him to see. For the first time, I felt myself breaking free from fear. I started to stand in the face of fear, and it felt good. For the first time since I was 14 years old, I felt free.

Little did I know that James taking the job with the church was just the beginning of my journey. It was the first time I would silence fear instead of being silenced by fear. I allowed myself to become a victim of fear rather than a volunteer to change it. I changed that day: I learned that we are not victims of fear, we are volunteers. Fear is a temptation, giving in to it is a choice. When you give in to fear you will feel trapped; you will feel like a slave, and you will feel like the only way to silence it is to give in to it. But those are all lies meant to silence you and the purpose you were created to fulfill.

I always thought that the fear I had was keeping myself and my family safe. I didn't know I was giving in to fear, and I didn't realize that I was making my whole family bow to the fear I had. I felt I needed fear. I felt safe with fear. I learned that my fear had nothing to do with my family or me–it had everything to do with fear having the power over me. Fear wasn't a warm blanket, it was chains of bondage.

Fear does not protect us–it binds us and holds us prisoner. We either give in to fear or we stand up to it. Fear is not what keeps us safe, it keeps us enslaved. Fear keeps us bowing in submission to it.

If we want to change the world for Jesus, then we have to change. We have to see fear for what it is: the enemy's tactic to silence us. We have to trust that God will never leave us or abandon us. He will stand in the fire with us! God has gone beyond being with us, he has equipped us with power. Fear is not from God; he doesn't use it against us or on us. God has given us power, love, and self-discipline to silence fear.

"For God has not given us a spirit of fear and timidity, but of power, love, and self-discipline."
2 TIMOTHY 1:7 NLT

We are a volunteer army. We are women created by God on purpose and for a purpose. We were created to change the world around us for Jesus.

Changing the world for Jesus starts when you silence fear and stand up for your faith. Stand up when everyone bows, stand up even if you stand alone, stand up even if...

Shadrach, Meshach, and Abednego thought they stood alone while the silenced army bowed, but they were never alone–God was with them the entire time.

When you choose to no longer be silenced by fear but instead choose to stand in the face of it, you are not alone. God is standing beside you. He stands next to you and says, "Now this is a girl I can change the world through."

3 SILENCED BY PAIN

We, the Christian women of this world, are a silenced army. Silenced by pain.

The pain of loss.
The pain of rejection.
The pain of abuse.
The pain of betrayal.

Pain brings us down to a bow with the weight of it. Pain can feel eternal and will leave you feeling exhausted, hopeless, and broken—like pieces of your life are scattered, never to be recovered and restored.

Pain will lie to you. It will tell you you're weak and broken. Pain will tell you that your life is over, and you will never be the same.

Pain will silence you. Pain will make you bitter, angry, and untrusting.

That is just what the enemy needs: an army silenced by pain, unwilling to move or act, untrusting and unable to stand.

I was 18 when I realized pain has many levels. My dad was controlling, untrusting, emotionally, verbally, and physically abusive my whole life, so I was no stranger to pain. But the pain I had gone through over the years was nothing in comparison to what was about to happen.

I walked into my house from the garage and into the laundry room. My dad was standing there furious, fists at his side and stiff as a board. He was angry. I knew that look in his eye and that stance, but I wasn't afraid. I stood there, looking him in the eye as he interrogated me as to where I had been, who I had been with, and what I had been doing. This was the routine, and I knew it well. In the past, I would answer the questions as timidly as possible, avoid eye contact, and answer each question carefully–doing my absolute best to keep from sounding like I was challenging him.

This time was different, because years of this type of treatment had given me courage. I looked my dad in the eye and answered all his questions truthfully, but without the cowering stance I knew he liked.

One minute I was talking, and the next minute I was on the floor. He struck me so hard with his fist across my face that my feet flew out from under me and down I went. I was caught off guard and didn't react fast enough to catch myself before my body and head hit the floor. Shocked and bleeding, I looked up at him and realized this was just the beginning.

I remember thinking, how does this end? Where do we go from here? How do I make this stop?

As I asked those questions in my mind, something changed. I immediately felt that this time was different. His eyes were distant, cold, hollow, and clouded. He was out of control. The next thing I remember is his firm grip on my throat and the slow tightening of his hand. I couldn't breathe. I couldn't fight. I couldn't talk. I couldn't scream. All I could do was look into his eyes and pray that he could stop himself, that God would stop him before my consciousness completely faded away. I thought to myself, *This is the end.*

God heard my thoughts as if they were prayers and answered me. Suddenly, my dad released me and watched as I gasped for air. I stumbled to my room and laid on my bed feeling numb—not a single tear, no pain, no anger, no fear—just a welcomed numbness that almost felt like peace.

Pastor and police officer, sworn to uphold the laws of God and the laws of the land—respected, admired, honored, and looked up to. My dad, my abuser. How am I supposed to reconcile that in my mind and in my heart? How do I tell everyone who thinks he is amazing that he isn't who you think he is? I didn't say a word. I was silenced by pain.

Days later, the numbness started to wear off, and every extra layer of makeup, every bruise, sore muscle, and cut was a reminder of my secret. A reminder of my pain. A reminder of my silence.

One night a few months later, as I was getting ready for bed, the pain of that memory came rushing in like a flood, with every feeling imaginable coming at me like a tidal wave. I felt panic rising up, threatening to swallow me up and never let me go.

In this moment of desperation, I felt like running—but to where? There wasn't a place on this earth that I could go where my memories and pain wouldn't follow me.

Right there in my bedroom, I kneeled on the floor and talked to God; I cried and I got angry. I blamed myself, blamed my dad, and blamed God. I didn't reconcile, I just wanted God to know where we stood. I was in pain and had no idea how to make it stop.

The enemy will try to convince you that you are alone in your pain and that no one will understand. He tells us our pain is unique to us, and that this burden is ours alone to carry. Then he shames us. He tells us we deserved it: We should have been stronger, we shouldn't feel this much pain, and we are weak. The list of lies goes on, playing and re-playing in our minds. His tactics begin to work, as we believe the lie day after day.

We bow to pain instead of standing up to it; we bury the pain deep and live with the shame of it. I realized no matter how deep you bury pain, it will always rise to the surface. Pain will taint everything it touches: marriages, family relationships, jobs, and your relationship with God.

Every time pain would rise to the surface, I would scold God. I had no one else to talk to, so God had to hear it all. He got my complaints, anger, hurt, fear, bitterness, resentment, and shame. Feeling bad for the way I was talking to God, I would angrily ask him "Who else am I supposed to talk to? The people at church, the one place I feel least accepted, least loved, with the people I trust the least? Of course not, so let's do what the rest of the world does and call the police. Oh wait, my dad is the police. Who will believe a teenage girl over one of their own in uniform?"

I felt alone and trapped in my pain, so day after day, I told God about it. Day after day, I yelled at God; day after day, I cried out to God. Even though all my physical wounds had healed, the wounds on my heart and mind were still open and bleeding.

Suffering on the inside, I was desperate for the pain to go away.

"A woman in the crowd had suffered for twelve years with constant bleeding.

She had suffered a great deal from many doctors, and over the years she had spent everything she had to pay them, but she had gotten no better.

In fact, she had gotten worse. She had heard about Jesus,

so she came up behind him through the crowd and touched his robe.

For she thought to herself, 'If I can just touch his robe, I will be healed.'

Immediately the bleeding stopped, and she could feel in her body that she had been healed of her terrible condition.

Jesus realized at once that healing power had gone out from him,

so he turned around in the crowd and asked, 'Who touched my robe?'

His disciples said to him,

'Look at this crowd pressing around you. How can you ask, 'Who touched me?"

But he kept on looking around to see who had done it.

Then the frightened woman, trembling at the realization of what had happened to her, came and fell to her knees in front of him and told him what she had done.

And he said to her,

'Daughter, your faith has made you well. Go in peace. Your suffering is over.'"

MARK 5:25-34 NLT

This unnamed woman, who was impoverished after spending all her money on a cure, had given up on hope. She was doomed to spend the remainder of her days in incredible pain from a condition that was getting worse by the day, condemned to spend the rest of her life isolated and plagued with rejection. She heard about Jesus and decided nothing was going to stop her from getting to him. Sickness, pain, rejection, hopelessness, loneliness, and desperation brought her to the crowd around Jesus.

She fought her way through the crowd that stood between her and her healing, emboldened and resolute with every step she took toward Jesus: She was going home healed. With faith stronger than her sickness and pain, she tells herself, *If I can just touch His robe, I will be healed.*

She didn't stand in line and wait her turn. She didn't explain her condition, and she didn't expect to be noticed. She had something precious—her faith. She knew that a simple touch of his robe would transfer his healing power to her broken body.

When I close my eyes, I can see the minute before her healing playing out. She is pushing through the crowd and sees Jesus. Excitement bubbles up in her heart. As she pushes urgently through the crowd, now she is mere inches from her healing, and she can barely stand it. With one last push toward Jesus, she reaches out with determination and touches his robe. She did it. She made it to Jesus. Standing still as the crowd pushes in around her, she closes her eyes as Jesus' pure healing power flows through her body, making her whole, healed, and set free.

Jesus stops. Touched not by a woman, but by her faith. He wants to talk to her.

Having lived a life of suffering, with hidden internal pain and external pain that has stolen her life from her, she resorts to fear–the same fear she has lived with most of her life. As Jesus calls for her, she realizes her body had been healed, but her mind was still locked in pain and fear.

Trembling and on her knees before Jesus, she tells her story, waiting to be scolded and rejected. Jesus with pride and love in his voice says, "Daughter, your faith has made you well. Go in peace. Your suffering is over." He healed not only her body but also her mind. He tells her "Go in peace." He fully healed her mind, body, and spirit. Her body had been healed when she reached out and touched Jesus' robe, but her mind still carried the wounds of a lifetime of sickness, rejection, hopelessness, pain, and hurt. Jesus saw her heart and saw the hurt, so he mercifully spoke directly to it: "Go in peace. Your suffering is over." These are my favorite words of her story. Jesus is speaking to you, saying: "My daughter, my precious girl, my love, my pride and joy: go in peace. Your suffering is over."

Jesus could have said, "I have made you well." He could have said, "You're welcome." But he didn't. He said, "Your faith has made you well." She stood for faith, and she silenced pain! This woman put action to her faith. She was tired of being sick and tired of suffering. She knew who could heal her, so she took steps for her healing. Instead of resigning to the pain, she was resolute in receiving her healing. Because of her faith, she got so much more than physical healing: She received complete healing of her mind and peace was restored to her heart and life. Jesus does not heal half of our pain; he heals it all. The body, the mind, and the spirit.

Pain will silence you, but there is another option–healing through Jesus.

Completely unaware of the healing that was happening every time I reached out to God, I began to feel peace after every tirade. I began to feel heard, healed, and closer to God. The closer I felt to God, the more I ran to him, and the more I ran to him, the less pain I felt. The nightmares steadily became less frequent, the hurt less sharp, and the memories less painful.

Then one day, the pain turned into determination. I was determined to heal; I didn't want my whole life to be the culmination of my worst day. I wanted that day to be just one day in a life well lived, full of joy, hope, peace, and freedom.

I pushed through the crowd, and I touched the robe of Jesus. Silenced no longer by pain, but instead pain was silenced. Once bowing to the pain, I slowly began standing to my feet, until I was standing tall. Now I see that I was never alone: Jesus was with me the entire time. He had been healing me every time I reached out to him. The pain of having no one to talk to was a blessing, because it left me with one option: Jesus.

I was no longer a victim of pain; I was a volunteer to replace it with healing.

Jesus, with pride and love in his voice, said to me, "Daughter, your faith has made you well. Go in peace. Your suffering is over." And he was right. Pain silenced.

Jesus was there every time I called out to him. He walked with me patiently, stopping when I stopped, walking when I walked, listening when I talked. He caught my tears when I cried and graciously allowed me to be angry, even when it was directed at him. I believe he was proud of me through the process, because no matter what our conversations looked like, I was talking to him through it all. The stripes Jesus took on his back and the beating he endured was for this reason. He saw my pain and gladly accepted the forty lashes so that one day the healing I needed was readily available–healing he knew I would need and come to him for. He gladly accepted every beating so I could be made whole. All of the pain he suffered was so I didn't have to live a life filled with pain. A gift paid with a high price, freely given to me.

"But he was pierced for our rebellion,
crushed for our sins.
He was beaten so we could be whole.
He was whipped so we could be healed"
ISAIAH 53:5 NLT

He can handle tough conversations and words said out of pain. It's when we reject him that his hands are tied. He needs you to come to him with faith—desperate, broken, hurting, shattered faith. He will pursue you, but if you continue to run, he can't heal you. He saw your pain and took the forty lashes so you could be made whole. A gift paid with a high price, freely given to you. He's waiting for you to reach out and touch his robe. With faith stronger than your pain you tell yourself, "If I can just touch his robe, I will be healed." With love in his voice and in his eyes, he allows healing to flow out of him and into you. Then he looks at you and says, "Go in peace. Your suffering is over."

"Then Jesus said, 'Come to me,
all of you who are weary and carry heavy burdens,
and I will give you rest.'"
MATTHEW 11:28 NLT

Healing you is his priority. He sees your life and future. He sees the life you will have if you keep your pain, and this life breaks his heart. It is filled with suffering, pain, loneliness, and heartbreak—a shattered and wasted life. He sees the life where you give your pain to him. He knows what will happen after you touch his robe. He sees healing, joy, freedom, purpose, confidence, and a life put back together by his masterful hands. He sees a life that will change the world—a life free of suffering.

Jesus doesn't see your pain when he looks at you. He sees your life without it.

Jesus doesn't see your brokenness when he looks at you. He sees your healed life.

Jesus doesn't see your hurt when he looks at you. He sees your life without it.

Jesus doesn't see your weaknesses when he looks at you. He sees his strength in you.

Jesus can see that the healing you experience on the other side of pain will become more than your story—it becomes your testimony. By standing up to pain and reaching for your healing, you become a walking and talking beacon of hope, a living and breathing symbol of healing, a banner for freedom, and an example of healing.

You can change the world for Jesus with your powerful story of God's healing and your submission and willingness to exchange your pain for peace, joy, and freedom.

Your life now becomes proof of this verse:

"And we know that God causes everything to work together
for the good of those who love God
and are called according to his purpose for them."

ROMANS 8:28 NLT

Your deepest hurt, your greatest suffering, and your crippling pain is now used by God to change the world. The enemy, who hopes to silence you with pain, is now defeated.

An army standing tall, unafraid, unmoved, confident, and expectant that through our story of healed pain, others will come to find the same hope and healing. By our example of reaching out for the robe of Jesus, you will give others the courage to do the same.

This is how we change the world for Jesus. We lead by example, by walking in freedom and healing, and we tell everyone who will listen. We don't bow to pain, we stand in the face of it—healed, made whole, and suffering no longer.

We, the Christian women of the world, are no longer silent. We are ready to share the healing power of Jesus with anyone in pain or who is suffering, bullied, rejected, depressed, abused, trafficked, enslaved, addicted, raped, and silenced in our world.

As long as there is sin, atrocities will continue to happen. Pain will be inevitable, but as long as one person is willing to stand up and share their story, there will always be hope. We are millions. We are able to share Jesus around the world with the same determination and courage that the woman who touched Jesus' robe had.

We are not powerless in this world; we are empowered. We will not bow; we will stand. We are not silenced; we are speaking out. We are not broken; we are healed. We are not alone; we have Jesus.

One Sunday morning while preaching, James shared my story. I sat there and listened to my story being told to me. It was such an amazing feeling to know that I have been healed of the pain that I thought would follow me my entire life.

On the way home from church that day, God gently reminded me to never forget what he has brought me through. If I forget what he has done, then I will forget to share the healing power of Jesus with others. I have been so wholly healed that for years I had forgotten that my story was now my testimony. A testimony that I am responsible to steward, share, speak, and give away as an offering to God for what he has done for me.

Hanging on to pain is a temptation, giving in to it is a choice. When you give in to fear you will feel trapped. You will feel like the only way to silence it is to give in to it, but those are all lies meant to silence you and the purpose you were created to fulfill.

If the enemy can't silence you with pain, he will gladly take any silence at all. Keeping your healing to yourself is just as damaging to the world around you as not being healed at all. Your healing is for you and all who will be brave enough to reach for Jesus' robe, because you had the courage and boldness to share your healing.

When you choose to no longer be silenced by pain, but instead choose to stand in the face of it, you are not alone. God is standing right beside you. He stands next to you and says, "Now this is a girl I can change the world through."

4 SILENCED BY DOUBT

We, the Christian women of this world, are a silenced army. Silenced by doubt.

Doubtful that we can make a difference.
Doubtful that we are enough.
Doubtful of our worth.
Doubtful of our purpose.
Doubtful of God's love.

Doubt is the thief of trust, hope, and faith. It will leave you feeling guarded and alone.

After James accepted the job with the church, I was feeling good for a while, but I was used to fear being a constant companion. When the chains of fear were gone, I felt like I needed to replace them with doubt. I doubted that God could protect my heart, or that God's plans for my life were good and not to harm me. I doubted that I could trust him.

James was happy in his new position with the church, because he was living out his purpose. He was right where God wanted him to be, and he glowed with fulfillment from the inside out. I was happy for him and happy that it was him and not me. I didn't want any of it for myself. As long as one of us had our feet on the ground, we would stay safe, remain whole, and keep our happy family intact. I was doubtful that God would keep us together; after all, he is a busy God with a whole lot of people under his care. My thinking was that I'd take one family (my family) off of his overflowing plate, and I'd take care of them myself.

I took care of our family while James served and worked at the church. I was completely content with just volunteering from time to time. That is when God came knocking. He was looking for a volunteer–me. I knew it was only a matter of time, but I was hoping for more time. I was happy where I was. I wasn't ready to admit that I doubted God, and I wasn't prepared to have my faith and trust pushed and tested.

James' responsibilities had expanded. He was leading multiple ministries and needed help with one of them, so he asked me. The church had a bookstore, and for many years before we had our kids, I was a retail manager. So naturally, he asked me to volunteer my time and experience. I politely, yet firmly declined not once, not twice, but three times over the period of a few months.

Then one Sunday, James and I were sitting in church listening to the message when our pastor said something that rocked my heart. I can't remember what he was preaching about, but I do remember the part that mattered–the part God used to bring me fully back to him and changed my life forever. He said our response to God should be: "God the answer is yes, now what's the question?" I knew that God was talking directly to me; I felt those words hit me in the deepest part of my doubt, rebellion, anger, selfishness, and fear. At that moment, I knew God was calling me to silence doubt. I didn't make eye contact with James, because I knew he would lift one eyebrow which means, "I told you so." I leaned toward him, and without looking at him, said, "Fine, I'll do it."

I would love to say that everything was smooth sailing from there, but it wasn't. God was about to make me face my doubt and lovingly show me how to trust him.

In my experience, doubt is worse than fear. Fear is for yourself; we use it to protect ourselves and to keep us safe. It's a selfish emotion. Doubt is a direct insult to God. It's as if we are saying, "I don't trust you," or maybe, "I don't fully trust you." It is a direct attack on the character of God. When we doubt him, we are telling him that whatever his plan, path, or purpose is for us, it isn't good enough. We unwittingly say, "God, I know better than you. My way can be trusted, and I choose any advice over yours. James 1:6 NIV puts it this way: *"The one who doubts is like a wave of the sea, blown and tossed by the wind."*

Doubt leaves you at the mercy of today's feelings. It anchors you to your feelings instead of to God, who has the solutions. God has an answer for every question, a solution to every problem, healing for every sickness, and mending for every brokenness. Doubt keeps us second guessing God and his ability to make all things new.

An army that doubts their leader is a silenced army.

We can't win without trust in our commander and leader. We are supposed to be an army united by God. We are supposed to be an army with the common goal of sharing Jesus with the world. We are supposed to be an army who wants the next generation to carry the message of Jesus forward. We are supposed to be an army that wants to stop and drown out the voice of the enemy with the message and righteousness of Jesus. We are supposed to trust our God wholeheartedly.

How are we supposed to do all this when we doubt him? How are we supposed to change the world for Jesus when we don't trust him to change us? How are we supposed to be his army when we doubt that through us, he can make a difference?

The answer is we don't. As a silenced army we bow down to doubt.

I mentioned how pushing past my doubt was hard–and when I say hard, I mean it was excruciating–but I was walking and talking with God through it all. I was making progress, and I know God was pleased with my efforts, because he is pleased with any and all efforts to trust him. Then came one of the biggest trust hurdles I have ever had to jump over. I wanted to blame God; I wanted to revert to my doubt, but I had come too far to go back to doubt.

When my daughter Nichelle was 5 years old, she had to have an MRI of her brain after having episodes of blindness. Nichelle was enjoying every moment of kindergarten, when about halfway through the year her life, and ours, changed forever. The phone rang: It was the school nurse. She said, "Nichelle says she is having trouble seeing." The nurse put Nichelle on the phone. I asked Nichelle a few more questions to get a better understanding of what was going on. Nichelle wasn't having trouble seeing–she was having episodes of blindness. And so, our journey began. That day it was determined that she would have a number of doctor appointments and see a whole gaggle of specialists that to this day we call the "ists." After a few fruitless attempts at getting to the bottom of what was going on, an MRI of her brain was ordered. We were told that no 5-year-old has ever stayed still for the hour-long MRI, and that Nichelle was going to be sedated. My little warrior girl was not having it.

Nichelle was adamant that she did not want to be sedated for the MRI; she promised she would stay still the entire time and was confident that the loud noises would not scare her. James and I decided to allow her to try. To prepare her, we would talk about the loud noises and practice thumbs up and thumbs down motions so we could communicate how she was feeling during the MRI. We spent the majority of our prep time talking about how much Jesus loves her and how she is never alone–NEVER! We would repeatedly tell her that even though we couldn't talk to each other during the duration of the MRI, Jesus would be there to comfort her. He would be with her the whole time.

We arrived at the hospital early in the morning. When we checked in, I found out I couldn't be in the room with her. Panic immediately filled my heart and mind. I was thinking of a million reasons why I needed to be in the room with her, but all that really made sense was that I wanted to be with her—I needed to be with her for my peace of mind. I told myself, *She needs me; I need to be with her.* James, Nichelle, and I walked into the room together and changed her into the little hospital robe. They put an IV in her small hand, just in case she needed sedation, and she put on headphones with Disney princess music playing. She hopped up on the bed, and after we said a little prayer together, she bravely said goodbye to me. I hugged her, squeezing her harder than I should have, and struggled to pull myself away from her.

She wasn't completely alone. James was with her, but as I mentioned earlier, I had taken my family off God's plate and James' plate. I was in charge of keeping my family healthy, safe, and happy. I thought I would be ok with allowing James to stay with her during this MRI since I was with her for all the other tests she had already gone through, but I was wrong.

I left the room with my heart pounding and my eyes burning from unshed tears. I prayed, "God, please be with my little girl," over and over while tears streamed down my face. That was the moment I was ready to silence the voice of doubt: God brought me to the place I needed to be. I needed to be in way over my head, and tapped out emotionally, I needed to be brought to a place where I knew I was not enough. I needed to be ready for him to take over. I knew that God could handle it and wanted to take the burden from me. The realization of how much I doubted God became crystal clear to me. All these years I had been protecting my family from God, I had no idea that all we needed was God and that one day, in the worst possible way, I would find this out. I knew I had allowed doubt to silence me. I looked doubt in the eye and said, "no more." I know who my enemy is—and it is not God.

The technicians saw my struggle and mercifully allowed me to stay in the tech room with them so I could watch Nichelle through the window. She did well. Just like we practiced Nichelle would slowly move her little thumb up to let her daddy and I know she was doing good, and every time she did, tears would stream down my face. She was doing ok, I was ok, and everything was going to be ok. I would tell myself this over and over to calm my anxious heart.

She got through the hour-long MRI perfectly; she never moved or cried, and she did it without sedation or me in the room.

A few weeks later, we were all together in the car taking Nichelle and our son Kyle to school. Kyle was telling us about a dream he had. He said, "I was singing a song about Jesus in my dream, but I had never heard this song before." James told him that Jesus speaks to us in many different ways, including dreams. Suddenly, Nichelle interrupts the conversation by saying, "Jesus talks to me." A knot formed in my throat making it impossible to speak, so James asked the question we were both thinking. "What does He say to you?" Her response was breathtaking. She said, "When I had my MRI, Jesus kept saying he loves me."

As I wrote this story, tears were streaming down my face, I can't help but cry every time I share this, because it is a sweet reminder of how much Jesus loves me and her. I was worried, upset, and anxious because I couldn't be in the room with Nichelle; I was smack dab in the middle of doubt when God showed up and rescued me. James wasn't the only one in the room with her: Jesus was there talking to her and reassuring her all the while. Jesus was with my little girl, even after I did my best to protect her from him.

The results of the MRI were not good, and we were about to face one of the hardest times in our lives. But God already knew that, and he was ready to endure with us. He knew what was to come, and that we couldn't do it without him. He allowed me to see the pain of doubt and going through it alone, and he allowed me to feel peace after I silenced doubt–the kind that can only come from complete trust in him.

That day, I learned that he loves each and every one of us individually, and that he can be trusted. He was there for his daughter Nichelle when she needed him. At the same time, he was there for me when I needed him. By telling my little girl that he loved her, he was telling me that she would never be alone, that he loved her more than I do, and when I teach her that she is never alone because Jesus is always with her, I shouldn't just say it, I should believe it as well.

I believed for my daughter, but I didn't believe for myself. I was silenced by doubt, but not anymore. Now I silence the voice of doubt. I know who my leader is, and I know he can be trusted. I know where he leads his army, I will follow, without a doubt. God is wanting us to trust him so he can help us, heal us, love us and lead us. I badly needed help when I was drowning in doubt, fear, and overwhelming emotions. The solution was silencing doubt and trusting God. It worked–God keeps his word, he doesn't lie. Silence doubt and allow God to help you.

"Commit everything you do to the LORD.
Trust him, and he will help you."
PSALM 37:5 NLT

It is easy to doubt God when you feel like you are one in 7.7 billion. To God, you are ONE, his one and only. He remains with you at all times: when things are good, bad, hard, happy, sad, disappointing, heartbreaking, exciting, joyful, or victorious. He will stay when others leave. He will be there when you are alone in your hurt. He will be there when you feel like you can't go on. He is there even when you doubt him. He is there when you are doubtful that you can make a difference, doubtful that you are enough, doubtful of your worth, doubtful of your purpose and calling, doubtful of God's love for you, and doubtful that his plans for you are good.

God so loves you! I know this to be true; I have experienced it, felt it, and accepted it. He doesn't deserve our doubt. He deserves blind trust and complete faith; he deserves to have an army that silences doubt. He deserves an army that is willing to stand when everyone bows and is willing to change the world for him.

You are an essential part of his plan: Your purpose is so important, that sometimes he will silence you to silence your doubt.

"Zechariah and Elizabeth were righteous in God's eyes, careful to obey all of the Lord's commandments and regulations. They had

no children because Elizabeth was unable to conceive, and they were both very old. One day Zechariah was serving God in the Temple, for his order was on duty that week. While Zechariah was in the sanctuary, an angel of the Lord appeared to him, standing to the right of the incense altar. But the angel said, 'Don't be afraid, Zechariah! God has heard your prayer. Your wife, Elizabeth, will give you a son, and you are to name him John.' Zechariah said to the angel, 'How can I be sure this will happen? I'm an old man now, and my wife is also well along in years.' Then the angel said, 'I am Gabriel! I stand in the very presence of God. It was he who sent me to bring you this good news! But now, since you didn't believe what I said, you will be silent and unable to speak until the child is born. For my words will certainly be fulfilled at the proper time.'"

LUKE 1:6-8,11,13,18-20 NLT

If we want to silence the voice of doubt, we have to silence the voice that speaks doubt. We all have that nay-sayer voice in our head, and if we let it, that voice will drown out God's voice.

In Luke chapter one, God was about to perform a miracle. This miracle was named John, and he would be the one to prepare the way for Jesus. The last thing God needed was the father of the miracle baby sharing his doubts with others. John needed the credibility of his heritage, not the doubting words from his father's mouth about paternity. Even the slightest doubt would have put John's mission and message at risk.

Your purpose is important but not more important than the mission. The mission is to change the world for Jesus, and that mission can't have doubting voices coming from the army which is supposed to deliver the message.

An army that silences the voice of doubt will unapologetically, boldly, and confidently bring the saving message of Jesus. This message will replace lies with truth, bring hope to the hopeless, healing to the sick and broken, joy to the depressed, peace to the anxious, direction to the lost, significance to the unseen, a hearing ear to the unheard, freedom to the enslaved, and Heaven to the hellbound. The voice that will be heard is the voice that trusts the leader, believes in the message, and silences the voice of doubt.

If we want to change the world for Jesus, we must not become victims of doubt but volunteers to change it. We must recognize doubt for what it is: a direct insult to God. It is saying, "I don't trust you," or maybe, "I don't fully trust you," and is an attack on the character of God. When we doubt him, we are telling him that whatever his plan is, wherever his path leads, whatever his purpose is for you, it isn't good enough.

Elizabeth had the same opportunity to doubt as her husband did, but she chose to stand when her husband bowed to doubt. She chose to trust God; she chose to believe.

"...his wife Elizabeth became pregnant and for five months remained in seclusion. She declared, 'The Lord has done this for me. In these days He has shown me favor...'"

LUKE 1:24-25 NIV

Elizabeth got to keep her voice. She was trusted to speak because she believed, and she gave the Lord credit. She declared, "The Lord has done this for me." She didn't just silence the voice of doubt–she didn't have any doubt, and she used her voice to declare trust. She lived an entire life waiting and trusting God, even though she felt disappointment month after barren month. According to human standards, she had every reason to doubt God, but she didn't. Instead, she silenced doubt and embraced trust–month after month, year after year, decade after decade. She silenced doubt until the day she held her newborn promise–her son.

God has systematically silenced the voice of fear and doubt in my life because he knew he had a message for me to preach, a ministry to build, and books to write. God needed me to trust him so through me he can change the world.

You may be part of the silenced army because you are struggling with trust. You know that you doubt God, but you can't bring yourself to trust him; so instead of being silenced by God, you have silenced yourself. You are not alone, and your doubts are not a disqualifier—they are a motivator for God to bring you to the place of trust. Don't fight the process or see your pain as a false reminder that God can't be trusted, but rather see it as a reason to silence the voice of doubt and choose to trust God.

The enemy wants you to live in doubt, because if he can keep you doubting God, he can stop you from trusting everything God says. He can prevent you from fulfilling your purpose and calling, and he can keep you locked in the army silenced by doubt. He can stop you from changing the world for Jesus.

You are not a victim of this sinful world: You are a volunteer to change it. You are not silenced by doubt: You are the silencer of doubt.

It is time to declare:
I trust you, God.
Through Christ, I can make a difference.
With Christ, I am enough.
Because of Christ, I am worthy.
I was created on purpose and with a purpose.
I am loved by God.
I was created to change the world for Jesus.

When you choose to no longer be silenced by doubt and instead choose to stand in the face of it, you are not alone. God is standing right beside you. He stands there next to you and says, "Now this is a girl I can change the world through."

5 SILENCED BY UNFORGIVENESS

We, the Christian women of this world, are a silenced army. Silenced by unforgiveness.

Unforgiveness is a slow-acting poison in your heart, soul, life, calling, and purpose.

Unforgiveness will slowly destroy your peace of mind, your health, your relationships, your trust in God, your reliance on faith, and your hope in Jesus.

The enemy knows the way to distract you from leading others to the forgiveness of Jesus is to keep you from forgiving. He tells us we should punish others with the lack of forgiveness, and we should make them pay for what they have done. They don't deserve forgiveness, and they don't deserve you. The enemy sits back and watches as you take these lies into your mind and heart; he watches as the poison slowly sets in and spreads. He watches as you slowly drop to your knees and bow to unforgiveness. He watches as you destroy your peace and happiness with unforgiveness.

"...when I forgive whatever needs to be forgiven,
I do so with Christ's authority for your benefit,
so that Satan will not outsmart us.
For we are familiar with his evil schemes."
2 CORINTHIANS 2:10-11 NLT

We are the voice of Jesus. We are supposed to take the message of forgiveness to an unforgiving and unforgiven world, but instead we harbor the enemy, and we harbor unforgiveness. We allow him to outsmart us with his evil schemes. We bow to unforgiveness willingly.

I was laying on my bed, feeling a welcomed numbness. I could not believe what had just happened–just minutes earlier I truly thought I was going to die, and now I was laying here alive and numb. Just then, my dad walks into my room, drops to his knees, and while crying hysterically, said, "I'm sorry but you made me do it." I stared at him in complete disbelief. Was this supposed to be an apology? Am I supposed to agree with him? Is he looking for an apology from me? *What is happening*? was all I could think before I decided I didn't want to find out; I just wanted the nightmare to end.

"I'm sorry but you made me do it," were the last words spoken that night. It would be another 18 years before that night was spoken of again.

In those 18 years while journeying through restoration, trust, and healing, I decided I wanted to forgive my dad. I decided that unforgiveness was a poison inside of me, killing only myself. I asked God to help me to forgive; I begged him to remind me of his forgiveness of my sin. I asked God to soften my heart so I would be able to wholeheartedly forgive my dad for the 18 years of mental, emotional, and physical abuse I endured while I lived under his roof.

To this day, forgiving my dad has been the hardest thing I have ever done. I didn't want to forgive him; I didn't want to allow my heart to soften to a man who had a hard heart. I didn't want to pray for my enemy, and I didn't want him to enjoy the gift of forgiveness when he never asked for it. I would like to say that the enemy was trapping me in unforgiveness, but that would be a lie. I hung on to it because I didn't want to let it go. I liked that anger and unforgiveness made me guarded–it gave me courage to look him in the eye when in the past I would have cowered. I liked that it gave me an excuse to be unkind and mean. I felt justified. I felt empowered. I felt strong. I liked unforgiveness–it felt good.

But it only felt good for a little while, and eventually the feeling started to bring me down to a bow. I knew that I was no longer in control of this feeling, it now controlled me. I began to panic because I was no longer in control and it amplified my feelings of helplessness, vulnerability, and fear. This was my breaking point.

My life, my relationship with Jesus, my family, and my happiness were too important to me to allow unforgiveness to steal a moment away from these priorities. I was determined to heal completely, and to accomplish that, I knew I needed to forgive. So, I worked on it, day and night, every day of every week of every month for years. Some days I was all about forgiveness; I could talk to him without feeling angry, and I could see him without feeling anxious and mad. I would think, *I finally did it—I forgave him*! Then other days, I saw him and all the old feelings would come flooding back; I would think to myself, *well I guess I haven't.*

God's patience with me, his forgiveness of my sin, and his process of healing the wounds on my body and heart taught me to be patient with myself in the forgiveness process. Be patient with the process, because it will not happen overnight. It won't be easy; it will be a struggle, but struggle does not mean failure. Struggle means you are working on it; it means you have not given up and God hasn't given up on you.

I took many breaks from seeing or talking to my dad for months at a time while I struggled to forgive him. I knew it would not happen overnight, but if I wanted to forgive and if I allowed God to work in the messiness of it, I would get there. Let God work in the messiness of unforgiveness, and let him be there to remind you when you are wallowing in unforgiveness to embrace the uncomfortable and irritating feeling of conviction. This process will bring you to healing and to forgiveness.

Unforgiveness is easy, because all you have to do is ride the wave of your feelings. You don't have to decide not to forgive, you just have to feed unforgiveness. You have to replay the offense over and over; you have to get mad over and over. You have to allow your sinful human nature to take over and take you wherever it wants to go. All you have to do is bow to unforgiveness, and it's yours for as long as you want it.

Forgiveness is hard. You have to discipline your mind and heart; you have to acknowledge that you chose unforgiveness, it didn't choose you. You have to fight your sinful nature and not allow it to take your life, your joy, and your heart. You have to stand up to unforgiveness, harness it, take it captive, and face it with Jesus. Facing unforgiveness is the hardest part. It hurts to look at it and realize unforgiveness didn't happen to you. Hurt, betrayal, abuse, neglect, and pain happened to you, but unforgiveness didn't. We pick up unforgiveness on our own, but when it starts to fester like an untreated wound, we blame the people that hurt us for it. We don't like taking responsibility for unforgiveness, and we rationalize it in our hearts by saying, "If they hadn't hurt me, I wouldn't have to forgive." That lie brings us down to a bow, and it holds us there.

We are not victims of unforgiveness: We are volunteers.

I decided to look unforgiveness in the eye and face it. I determined to put all the energy I was investing into unforgiveness and put it toward forgiveness. I had to put this into practice over and over again—I had to persevere and not give up or give in. Most people are looking for the quick fix to forgiveness; however, I have found that it is a long journey, and it entails forgiving the person or people that hurt you over and over again.

Even though, in reality, the abuse I suffered was over, my heart and head didn't want to let it go. I would involuntarily replay the scene in my mind and each time I had to say to myself, "I forgive you dad." There were times when tears would stream down my face when I said these words and other times through gritted teeth, but I said them every time I would feel the grips of unforgiveness around my heart.

I wanted to heal from the trauma of my life more than I wanted to hang on to unforgiveness.

I wanted wholeness, I wanted peace, and I wanted to forgive. I wanted to win by forgiving. I realized that harboring unforgiveness was a way of holding on to the past, and I wanted to be completely free of my past. The only way to freedom was through forgiveness.

"Then Peter came to him and asked,
'Lord, how often should I forgive someone who sins against me? Seven times?'
'No, not seven times,' Jesus replied, 'but seventy times seven!'"
MATTHEW 18:21-22 NLT

I had to forgive 70 times seven; I had to discipline my mind and emotions to forgive. I am forgiven daily of so much; I am loved even though I break God's heart. I have run from God, doubted God, and allowed fear and pride to be bigger than God. I rejected God and his plan for my life, yet he forgave me every time. He repeatedly forgives me even though I continue to sin and break his heart. He did this because he loves me, but also as an example of what true forgiveness looks like.

You are to forgive 70 times seven. You have to discipline your mind and emotions to forgive. You are forgiven daily of so much; you are loved even though you break God's heart. You have run from God, doubted God, rejected God, and allowed doubt and fear to be bigger than God. Yet he has forgiven you every time; he repeatedly forgives you even though you continue to sin and break his heart. He does this because he loves you! God wants you to see how he forgives so you will forgive as well.

We, the Christian women of this world, silenced by unforgiveness.

We feel justified. We feel empowered. We feel strong. We like unforgiveness. It feels good.

But, only for a while–eventually these feelings start to bring us down to a bow. We are no longer in control of these feelings, but instead they now control us. Unforgiveness is keeping us tethered to the past, and it blinds us to our future and the purpose God has for us. Unforgiveness will trap us in a maze of memories, it binds us with shackles of emotions, and keeps us from giving or accepting forgiveness.

The enemy will use the trauma of your life to keep you from forgiving so he can keep you from being forgiven.

"If you forgive those who sin against you,
your heavenly Father will forgive you.
But if you refuse to forgive others,
your Father will not forgive your sins."

MATTHEW 6:14-15 NLT

I used to hate this scripture, because it left no room for my special circumstance, my hurt, and my pain. It left no room for unforgiveness. I wanted a way to hang on to unforgiveness and still be forgiven. I wanted God to take away the pain of unforgiveness while allowing me to still hold on to it. This scripture makes it crystal clear how forgiveness works. He makes it clear so we don't misunderstand the importance of forgiveness. His desire is to forgive us. That is why he sent Jesus to die for us, but just as important, he wants us to forgive each other. God takes forgiveness seriously. He knows it will set you free, and he knows it has set you free.

God sent his only Son to die for our sins so we could have forgiveness at the drop of a prayer, spoken from a heart of repentance.

Living a life free from unforgiveness is beautiful. It allows us to see the hurt of the world through the lenses of forgiveness, to see another's pain instead of our own. It frees us up from feeling sorry for ourselves when we see their pain. Instead of comparing our pain, we compare our healing to their pain. That comparison inspires us to introduce them to Jesus; the One who can rescue them from their pain, and the One who can lead them to forgiveness and freedom.

We are not victim of unforgiveness: We are volunteers to forgive.

We, the Christian women of the world, volunteer to forgive those who have hurt us, abandoned us, neglected us, betrayed us, abused us, belittled us, used us, forgotten us, ignored us, humiliated us, and those who did not defend us. We forgive so we can be forgiven, and we forgive because we have been forgiven. We forgive so we can have freedom, and so we can share the power of forgiveness with a world that has bowed to unforgiveness. We forgive because we know the short-term pain of forgiveness is better than a lifetime of pain caused by unforgiveness. We choose to walk in the freedom paid for on the cross by our Savior.

We are the army of God–the army that marches with the banner of forgiveness. With confidence, we pray for forgiveness for our sins against you because we have forgiven those who have sinned against us.

"and forgive us our sins, as we have forgiven those who sin against us."

MATTHEW 6:12 NLT

I lived with the freedom and confidence of extending forgiveness to my dad, even though he never asked for it. Then one day, I got a call from my dad. This call put forgiveness to the test, and it stretched me to my limits. It brought me to the feet of Jesus with prayers to help me forgive, once again.

My dad was in rehab for alcoholism and one of the steps was to make amends with the people he hurt. Somewhere along my dad's journey to sobriety, he was reminded of the abuse I suffered at his hands. He called me to "make amends," in the only way a person who has never taken responsibility for abuse at his hand can. The conversation went like this:

"Nichole, I was told I have to call you to make amends as part of the 12-step program I am in. I've been told that I used to beat you. Is this true?" The pain those word brought were intense and immediate. My mind was searching for the words to say. I knew I needed to respond, but my mouth wouldn't form words. Years of Jesus and forgiveness helped me get the next words out. I said, "Yes, you did." Little did I know blow number two was a millisecond away. He began crying and through sobs he responded, "I did? How could I do something like that, I don't think I could do something like that, why did I do that, I can't believe I did that." That was his attempt at an apology. He never said he was sorry, he never tried to make amends, and he never admitted to the abuse. I had a choice to make now. I could have bowed under the weight of pain to unforgiveness or I could stand with the strength I had through Jesus. Jesus met me in that moment and covered me in peace, inspiring my next words. I said, "Dad, even though you have never asked for it, I forgave you a long time ago, and I forgive you now." There was silence for a while, and through tears, he said he had to go.

Both my husband and I worked for a church in Florida at the time. I walked into the office we shared and broke down. I cried the way I should have cried the night it all happened. My dad's "make amends" call brought back the pain, memories, and the temptation of unforgiveness. I felt re-victimized, and I felt strength seeping out of me. I so badly wanted to give in to anger and unforgiveness, but I knew I had come too far to go back; I knew the sting of unforgiveness and the freedom of forgiveness. I knew that God was calling me into obedience once again, and he was calling me to forgive.

After a good cry in my husband's arms, we prayed together, and once again, I went on the very short journey of forgiveness. This time I knew what I was doing and started immediately. This time I was prepared. Once again, I forgave my dad even though he never asked for it. Once again, I was free. I am free of unforgiveness because I believe every word of this scripture:

"Don't worry about anything; instead, pray about everything.
Tell God what you need, and thank him for all he has done.
Then you will experience God's peace,
which exceeds anything we can understand.
His peace will guard your hearts and minds as you live in Christ Jesus."

PHILIPPIANS 4:6-7 NLT

When I am feeling overwhelmed, angry, hurt, sad, or feeling the lure of unforgiveness beckoning me, every single time and without fail, I recite this scripture. I replace the thoughts I'm having with this prayer, and I put into practice these simple steps.

1. Don't worry about anything. Instead.
2. Pray about everything.
3. Tell God what you need.
4. Thank him for all he's done.

These four steps unlock the peace you are so desperately craving. I know from experience that if you genuinely follow the scriptures, THEN you will experience God's peace. His peace cannot be taken away from you–it can't be refuted and it can't be argued. He gives it to you as a gift. You get to own peace, enjoy it, and bask in it. But God is a God of above and beyond, and he takes it a step further. He says, *"His peace will guard your hearts and minds as you live in Christ Jesus."*

His peace will stand guard at the entrance of your heart and mind; his peace will not allow unforgiveness, anger, or hurt inside. His peace will keep your heart at peace.

It took me years to forgive my dad the first time, but the second time around, the peace of God was fighting on my behalf. After a good cry and implementation of the four steps above, I was not a victim of unforgiveness but a volunteer to forgive.

We were created on purpose and with a purpose. We were created to change the world around us. We were not created to be changed by the world, or our circumstances, or experiences. We were not created to sit in pain and wallow in unforgiveness, and we were not created to bow and be immobilized by the pain of our past and our unwillingness to forgive. We are not defined by what happened to us, but by our willingness to forgive.

God has a plan to reach the world through us, but he needs us whole, healed, redeemed, restored, forgiven, and forgiving so he can change the world for him through us. This unforgiving world needs to see Jesus through our forgiveness, and it needs to know that there is the hope of forgiveness through Jesus no matter what they have done. They need to know that the women of God's army will not judge or condemn them for their past but instead lead them to the one who wants to forgive them.

"But if we confess our sins to him,
he is faithful and just to forgive us our sins
and to cleanse us from all wickedness."
1 JOHN 1:9 NLT

Forgiveness received is a free gift: an undeserved gift but freely given.
Forgiveness given is a free gift: an undeserved gift but freely given.

When you choose to no longer be silenced by unforgiveness but instead choose to stand in the face of it, you are not alone. God is standing right beside you. He stands next to you and says, "Now this is a girl I can change the world through."

6 SILENCED BY SHAME

We, the Christian women of this world, are a silenced army. Silenced by shame.

We humans have a sin problem. We are stubborn, prideful, selfish, fearful, doubtful, lazy, addicted, jealous, and deceitful. I can go on and on so let's just call it like it is–sinful.

"For everyone has sinned;
we all fall short of God's glorious standard."
ROMANS 3:23 NLT

You may not struggle with fear or with doubt, but this verse puts us all in the same category of sinner.

A silenced army: every single one of us volunteers, every single one of us sinners.

An army plagued with the aftermath of sin, silenced by shame, guilt, worthlessness, and brokenness. This is an army stripped of its weapons and replaced with weights and chains.

This is not an accident: This is a strategic move by our enemy. A plan tried and true throughout the ages.

Satan targeted Eve because she was the missing piece in his plan. She was the piece he needed to bring sin into our world. He needed her to bring shame on an entire gender so we would become a silenced army. An army reminded of sin and shamed because of it. The ashamed army is an ineffective army, an immobile army, a scattered army—it is a silenced army.

Eve wasn't his only target of our gender. You are a target. You and your purpose to change the world for Jesus. You and your story of surrender to Jesus—your admission of sin and acceptance of his forgiveness. You and your voice. You and your willingness to act when your purpose and the need for it collide.

You are a target.

Satan doesn't need you to bring sin into the world; he needs you to be silenced by the sin in your world. He knows a silenced army allows battles to be won without a fight, and it will enable them to be surrounded and made to comply. A silenced army can only sit around and complain to an empty room about the battles being lost, the ground that's being taken, and the treasures that are being stolen.

Jesus saw our sin and went to the cross as a volunteer. He stood up and said, "I will pay the price. I will take on their shame, guilt, brokenness, and sin. I will bear the burden, so they don't have to." Jesus knew the burden would be too much for us to carry. He knew the weight of sin and shame would make us bow to them. Jesus was not a victim of the cross, he was a volunteer so that we wouldn't have to be victims of sin and shame, but volunteers to change it.

"No one can take my life from me. I sacrifice it voluntarily. For I have the authority to lay it down when I want to and also to take it up again."

JOHN 10:18a NLT

He prepared the way for The Army. The Army that would change the world for him.

For some, what Jesus did for us isn't good enough, so we choose to carry the shame of sins, both forgiven and forgotten; we decide to feel the shame of sins Jesus died to erase. We choose to be silenced and weighted down to a bow by the sin Jesus volunteered to die for.

We carry it in our hearts, allowing it to break us over and over, and we wrap the chains of guilt and shame around us like a blanket refusing to let it go. All the while Satan watches and thanks us for silencing ourselves.

How can we change the world around us when we don't accept the change in us? How do we offer the gift of forgiveness when we haven't received it? How can we teach grace when we refuse it? How can we teach others about the importance of the cross and Jesus' sacrifice when we don't see it ourselves?

How do we tell the lady who has had an abortion that Jesus forgives her and loves her when you haven't accepted the same gift of forgiveness?

How do you tell the young girl who feels invisible, worthless, ugly, and bullied that she is a masterpiece, created by God on purpose and with a purpose if you don't believe that for yourself?

How do you tell the addict that Jesus can set them free when you carry the weight and chains of your own shame, and you haven't embraced your freedom?

The short answer. We stay silent. Silent for fear we will be called hypocrites, liars, frauds, and fakes. Silenced by sin and shame.

Your real enemy is not shame, guilt, worthlessness, and brokenness—your real enemy is Satan. He uses these things to distract you and it's working. He knows we are not victims of these things; he knows we have the option of freedom at the speed of one prayer. He knows these are feelings, not conditions. He sees it for what it is: He knows we are volunteers and hang on to these feelings even though we don't have to.

Satan knows Jesus died on the cross to free us from these feelings. He was there, and he saw what Jesus did. Satan knows freedom is found in

Jesus, and he knows that you are so close to finding out that you don't have to live this way, so he whispers reminders of your past and present to you. If you choose to listen you have been effectively silenced.

Jesus will never bring shame or guilt into your life. He gives freedom, forgiveness, hope, healing, and restoration freely to all who ask.

"Jesus returned to the Mount of Olives, but early the next morning he was back again at the Temple. A crowd soon gathered, and he sat down and taught them.

As he was speaking, the teachers of religious law

and the Pharisees brought a woman who had been caught in the act of adultery.

They put her in front of the crowd.

'Teacher,' they said to Jesus, 'this woman was caught in the act of adultery.

The law of Moses says to stone her. What do you say?'

They were trying to trap him into saying something they could use against him, but Jesus stooped down and wrote in the dust with his finger.

They kept demanding an answer, so he stood up again and said,

'All right, but let the one who has never sinned throw the first stone!'

Then he stooped down again and wrote in the dust.

When the accusers heard this, they slipped away one by one, beginning with the oldest, until only Jesus was left in the middle of the crowd with the woman. Then Jesus stood up again and said to the woman, 'Where are your accusers?

Didn't even one of them condemn you?'

'No, Lord,' she said.

And Jesus said, 'Neither do I. Go and sin no more.'"

JOHN 8:1-11 NLT

What a powerful picture of grace. During that time if a woman was caught in adultery the only consequence was death. She must have been terrified as they put her in front of the crowd and asked the man who was teaching if she should be stoned. Can you imagine standing there dreading the words to come and the death sentence to follow?

The Bible doesn't say what her reaction was. But I can imagine silent tears were running down her face. Her heart must've been beating so hard she could hear it in her ears, and her hands shaking and her knees weak as she pleaded in her heart for mercy. But she didn't dare ask because she knew the law; she was guilty, and she knew everyone there thought she deserved this punishment. She knew she deserved it. I'm sure each second that passed felt like hours as she waited for this man to judge her and find her guilty, this man who was now stooped down writing in the dust with his finger as if entirely uninterested.

She listened as the men who brought her to Jesus grew more agitated, as they demanded an answer, as they demanded he speaks the words that condemned her to death–the words everyone except her were waiting to hear.

Then Jesus stood up. He stood up with the guilty woman, and he stood up for the guilty woman. He stood up to her accusers and said, "All right, but let the one who has never sinned throw the first stone!" Then he went back to writing in the dust.

I can imagine confusion was her first reaction and a glimmer of hope was her second–followed by humility and gratitude. Did this man really just stand up for me? Did he really defy the religious leaders? Is he truly offering mercy instead of death?

After all of her accusers had walked away, Jesus stood again. He looked at this guilty and shamed woman and asked, "Where are your accusers? Didn't even one of them condemn you?"

She was looking into the eyes of someone who should have been one of her accusers; he should have condemned her, yet here she is standing with this man who had mercy on her having a conversation like she was guilt-free, clean, and sinless.

With a shaky voice she answers him with a simple, "No, Lord." This guilty woman never expresses remorse, never apologized or tried to explain her side of the story, and she never even begged for mercy or promised never to sin again. Jesus in all of his grace, love, and mercy tells her, "Neither do I. Go and sin no more."

Jesus said to the guilty and shamed woman, I do not condemn you, you are set free. Jesus knows our heart; he knows who we are on the inside. I believe he saw this woman's heart and saw she was repentant, so he forgave her and released her from sin and shame.

"If we confess our sins to him,
he is faithful and just to forgive us our sins
and to cleanse us from all wickedness."

1 JOHN 1:9 NLT

She saw firsthand his faithfulness to forgive, but she was still guilty. His forgiveness didn't erase time and her memory, so how could she not be condemned for her sin?

"I will forgive their wickedness and will remember
their sins no more."

HEBREWS 8:12 NIV

He forgave her and remembered her sin no more. He stood with a woman free of sin, guilt, and shame. She was made new and whole in the eyes of Jesus.

"Finally, I confessed all my sins to you
and stopped trying to hide my guilt.

I said to myself, 'I will confess my rebellion to the LORD.' And you forgave me! All my guilt is gone."

PSALM 32:5 NLT

Jesus silenced sin and shame.

The enemy comes to you day and night judging you for your sin, bringing out of the shadows all of your mistakes, fears, doubts, insecurities, brokenness, guilt, and sin. He parades them in front of your worse accuser—YOU. You play back the scenes that have rendered you guilty, and you sentence yourself to a life of shame and silence.

Jesus stood upright on the cross for all to see, and he did it for you. On that cross, he stood up with you, he stood up for you, and he stood up to your accusers. The second you asked Jesus to forgive you, he accepted your plea and forgave you. From that moment on, he sees a forgiven, clean, whole, and healed woman, with not an accuser in sight. His sacrifice gave us the freedom to no longer live as victims of sin, but volunteers to be free of guilt and shame.

Silence the voice of shame. The battle is real, and it needs you. You were created by God on purpose and for a purpose. You were created to change the world around you for Jesus.

We, the Christian women of the world, have been given freedom. We are no longer silenced by sin and shame; instead, we are the front line of hope, we are the face of healing, and we are the voice of Jesus on earth.

The message of Jesus will replace lies with truth, bring hope to the hopeless, healing to the sick and broken, joy to the depressed, peace to the anxious, direction to the lost, significance to the unseen, a hearing ear to the unheard, freedom to the enslaved, and Heaven to the hellbound.

We are the forgiven and free, the healed and restored, the unashamed and unafraid, bringing the message of Jesus to the lost and bound, broken and sick, the ashamed and afraid, and the accused and condemned.

We can't be afraid or ashamed to bring these rare and precious gifts to a world that so badly needs them. With a shame-free life, we are required to share all that God can and will do for our world, and we have to use the shame-free voice we have been given with courage and boldness.

I grew up with a Jesus-loving, serving, dedicated, sold-out, faith-filled mom. I watched as she was ordained as a pastor, and as she shared the gospel of Jesus in church, outside the church, in living rooms, at the park, and just about anywhere she had a listening ear.

I thought this was normal, until I found out that there are those who don't believe in women pastors or women who preach in a church with a mixed-gender audience. I was shocked. I started asking the question, "Isn't the message we share more important than the gender of the messenger?" I got conflicting answers from multiple people of various religious backgrounds. I sat silently with a message burning in my soul wanting to come out, but I chose not to offend and instead chose silence.

Years later, when James and I were pastoring a church together, he told me, "You were created to preach the message of Jesus, it's time for you to start." I hesitated, but I knew he was right. I hesitated, because the years I chose silence were the years I allowed shame to seep into my heart—shame for my desire to preach, shame for being a female who wants to preach, and shame for choosing silence when I was purposed to speak. The enemy flooded my mind with the thoughts and echoed the voice of my dad in my mind telling me, "You're just a girl, you don't know what you are talking about. Who do you think you are?"

The persistent opposing questions kept coming back, begging me to find the answers. Am I supposed to share the message God has put in my heart? Can people be wrong?

If I preach will I offend people? If I don't preach, will I offend God?

The moment I said "yes" to James, all the worry, shame, fear, and doubt was gone. I knew at that moment my purpose was to teach and preach. I knew my purpose was to share the messages God put in my heart.

James was gracious in my request for us to preach together for my first time. That Sunday morning, I woke up with a terrible case of the stomach flu. The terrible kind where you don't leave the bathroom for any reason. I asked James if I could skip this time, and in the kindest tone of voice, he said, "no." I have no idea how I made it through the next three services, but by the grace of God, I did. Fortunately, I don't remember much: It was all a blur of nerves, fever, and the stomach flu. A few months later, he asked me to preach again. This time I was ready and healthy. I was shaky in my delivery, because I was a tad bit nervous and a whole lot excited. But James was right–this is what I was created to do.

I continued to preach, improving each time and loving it a bit more after every sermon. Just as I was finding my stride and confidence, my computer died days before I was supposed to preach. The message I had prepared was gone. We rushed my laptop to the Apple store, hoping they could retrieve something–anything at all–but to my heartbreak, it was all gone.

I lost a half-written book, all my past messages, and the message I was supposed to preach in just a few days. I'll admit I cried just a little bit. This all happened around Christmas time, and I hadn't put any Christmas decorations out yet, so I decided to put up our Christmas tree to cheer me up and take my mind off of my heartache and frustration.

I put up my first tree, wrapped it in lights, then called the whole family in the room to watch as I plugged in the lights. I couldn't wait for the lights to twinkle with holiday spirit. As the family stood there humoring me, I excitedly said, "Drumroll please." The family obliged, and I plugged in the lights. Silence. Nothing. No twinkling lights, no clapping, no joy, just my son's quiet voice saying, "Oh mom." Unshed tears stung my eyes as I walked outside to sit on the bench on our front porch to allow the fresh air to cool my emotions. I was feeling sorry for myself, unmotivated and reluctant to start rewriting the message I was supposed to preach. I couldn't keep the thoughts of shame from flooding in: Maybe *this is a punishment, maybe I'm not supposed to preach, maybe I am offending God. Maybe my dad was right and I am just a girl, unworthy, in the way, an inconvenience.*

I recognized the voice of the enemy: It is ugly, hurtful, and hateful. It is meant to intimidate into silence. I refused to listen. I refused to be silenced.

With only one day before I had to stand before the church and preach, I had nothing prepared. I sat in my office with the daunting task of starting over. I began to write, and it began to flow. It was a different message than the lost one, but I was ok with that.

I preached the message God gave me. I preached a message as new to me as it was to the audience. After the services, a young girl came up to me and shared her story. With a straight face and dullness in her eyes, she told me she was recently sexually molested by a family member. She shared how she immediately went to her parents with this information and was devastated when they told her they didn't believe her. She told the whole story without any emotion until she quoted a portion of my message back to me. Her voice cracked with emotion as she said; "God hears you; he sees your pain, he knows what has happened to you, he believes you, and he will heal you." She told me she needed to hear that, she needed to know someone believed her.

We sat together for an hour as I listened. When she was talked out, I shared with her some simple truths about Jesus' love for her, that he will never doubt her, leave her, or abandon her. I shared this from a place in my heart that was shame-free and guilt-free. I spoke from experience, and I badly wanted to take my healing and put it inside of her. However, I knew her only hope was Jesus. I spoke from firsthand experience of God's love and healing power. I wasn't trying to sell Jesus to her; I was sharing Jesus with her, and I was sharing hope with her.

If the enemy can't use your past to silence you, he will use your present—your insecurities, your fears, your doubts, and your feelings to silence you. If the only reason to silence the shame of being a female preacher and boldly stepping into my purpose and onto the stage to preach the message of Jesus was for that young girl, then it was worth it.

Shame in all its forms holds us back. It silences us and bottles up the purpose inside of us and locks it away.

No more. We will no longer be silenced.

We, the Christian women of this world, have to silence the voice of shame and guilt. We must wholeheartedly accept that Jesus stood upright on the cross for all to see, and he did it for us. On that cross, he stood up with us, he stood up for us, and he stood up to our accusers. This message, purpose, and calling that is rooted in our hearts has to be shared with the world.

The battle is real, and we are all needed in it. Shame cannot be the reason we choose to not step into our purpose, not when Jesus took our shame and bore it for us. We are forgiven, guilt-free, shame-free, set free, redeemed, and delivered. We are not victims of shame, instead we are volunteers to silence it–free to use our voice to share freedom with a world chained to shame.

When you choose to no longer be silenced by sin, shame, and guilt, and instead choose to stand in the face of it, you are not alone. God is standing right beside you. He stands there next to you and says, "Now this is a girl I can change the world through."

7 SILENCED BY OFFENSE

We, the Christian women of this world, are a silenced army. Silenced by offense.

Offended by the church.
Offended by the pastor.
Offended by people.
Offended by God.

I recently heard a speaker say that women today are balancing on a three-legged stool. The first leg represents their family, the second leg represents their faith, and the third leg represents their career. If she doesn't balance correctly, she will come crashing down.

She: the wife, mom, sister, daughter, aunt, grandma, caregiver.

She: the overworked, underappreciated, stressed-out, stretched thin, overcommitted, and overlooked woman.

I see this balancing act more and more by single moms, married moms, single ladies, married ladies, divorced moms, divorced ladies, widowed moms, and widowed ladies. The list of circumstances a lady now has leaves the church struggling to keep up and asking the question, "How do I speak to every single one of these scenarios in one hour, once a week?"

The answer is... they can't.

The latest research shows that this is affecting women's attendance to church. Women are choosing not to attend at all, because she no longer fits into the traditional role talked about in church.

Women are feeling slighted, overlooked, marginalized, forgotten, and underrepresented in the church, and they choose to be offended. Tired of only being offered volunteer positions in the nursery or kids' ministry, she protests by not volunteering at all. Tired of not seeing her gender represented on the stage, she protests with her generosity. Tired of not hearing a message tailor-fit for her, she protests with her attendance.

The world tells us that women have shattered the glass ceiling, while the perception is that church women are dealing with a dropped ceiling.

Women silenced by offense. They are comparing the church to the world and finding the church falls short.

She watches as a sea of pink shirts march in unison and unity for a cause. They are making noise, and they are heard. They are a community, with strength in numbers. They are not alone, as they walk arm in arm with strangers as if they were the best of friends.

She walks into a church where women are sitting alone in their loneliness, hurt, and brokenness. She wonders, *Where are all the pink shirts? Where do I fit in? Where are the people like me*? She leaves, vowing never to return.

Silently, thousands of ladies just like her leave empty seats in churches around the world.

Silenced by offense.

Silenced by offense will find everything wrong with the church, while those who silence offense will find everything right with the church.

She: the wife, mom, sister, daughter, aunt, grandma, caregiver.

She: the hardworking, works out when stressed out, multitasker-extraordinaire, committed, bold, determined, and courageous woman.

The world tells us that women have shattered the glass ceiling, but all she sees is the damage that the falling glass leaves behind. The collateral damage of pitting women against men, women against women, and men against men—all in the name of progress. Meanwhile, the perception is that church women are dealing with a dropped ceiling; however, she doesn't see a ceiling, she sees clear blue skies made by her creator. She sees endless possibilities to serve her community and to change the world around her for Jesus.

Women silencing offense.

She compares the church to the world and finds the church to be a safe place, a refuge, and a comfort. She sees the world for what it is: cold and unforgiving, judgmental, superficial and distracting.

She watches as a sea of pink shirts march in unison and unity for causes that break the heart of Jesus, causes that break her heart. They are making noise, and they are heard, but at what cost? They are a community brought together by their fight for their right to be wrong. While they are not alone, they don't have God. They have strength in numbers and can change the world—but then again, so can we.

She walks into a church where women are sitting alone in their loneliness, hurt, and brokenness, waiting to be comforted by the words of the songs to come and inspired by the message preached. No pink shirts here, just badges that say "welcome." You never have to ask where you fit in, because everyone fits in, and everyone is there for the same reason—to have an encounter with God, to learn and grow, to be encouraged, motivated, and challenged, and healed and heard by God. Everywhere you look there are people just like her.

She leaves, vowing to return.

Silently, thousands of ladies just like her fill empty seats in churches around the world.

In my younger years, I didn't love the church–I resented it. As the pastor's daughter, I felt watched continuously and critiqued. The pressure to be as close to perfect as a human can possibly get sat like a boulder on my chest, making it hard to breathe.

Just about every Sunday something was said to me that was offensive, whether it be about my dad, mom, or myself. I so badly wanted to run, so I found an acceptable way of running that didn't require me to actually run. On Sunday afternoons, between the morning and evening services, I would get in my car and drive as far out of town as time would permit. If I had three hours before I had to be back at church, I would drive an hour and a half out of town, then turn around and drive the hour and a half back.

I was not a victim of the church or offense; I was a volunteer. I clung to the idea that being offended allowed me to view church as miserable. Offense made it acceptable to fake a cough so I could skip church, and it made rude and bad behavior justifiable. It made me feel better about resenting church and resenting God.

Skip ahead fifteen years: James is working for a church, and even though I was happy, James was happy, and the kids were happy, my old habit of offense was hanging on. I found myself looking for reasons to be offended. Now let's be honest, because the church is full of people and run by people, offense isn't hard to find. The borderline offenses were easy to make full-blown offenses with just a little bit of a nudge, so offense was plentiful. The obvious offensive things that were said to me were gladly accepted and added to my growing list of everything that is wrong with the church.

God revealed this weakness to me, and I went kicking and screaming toward silencing offense. The journey toward silencing offense was moving along at a nice, slow pace when God sped up my journey by a thousand times to show me the beauty of the church.

Our daughter Nichelle was having periods of blindness as I shared in chapter four. The MRI revealed that she had a fibroma in her brain. This fibroma was a result of a condition called neurofibromatosis. The symptoms of this condition are as varied as the person who has it. There isn't a cure, and they can only treat the symptoms that develop as a result.

My heart ached day in and day out as each test and MRI resulted in more bad news. Nichelle's little body was struggling to keep up with not only the neurofibromatosis (or NF), but also complex migraines, severe environmental allergies, food allergies, staph infections, and eczema that covered her whole body, just to name a few things. Because of the stress on her body, she stopped growing. She was losing her hair and was pale and exhausted. Her little body in the constant grip of pain was more than this momma could stand. I prayed as I had never prayed before; I had more faith during this time than all the faith of my life combined. We would repeatedly tell Nichelle that God can and will heal her, and she believed us. We believed.

One weekend, our pastor asked if he could share what we were going through with the church so he and the church could pray for us. At that time, our church had six services, each filled with 1,000 people. The first service James and our pastor stood on the stage, and the church stood with them as our pastor prayed. They stood with us and for us; they stood silently as a church. I stood in the back of the church, tears streaming down my face as I watched the church, the one I chose to be offended by, now standing together and praying for my little girl.

I was taken aback by the silence broken only by the prayers of one man but agreed with by thousands. There were no chants, no bobbing signs, and no marching. There was the powerful roar of silent prayers, and all for one little 6-year-old girl who was believing for her miracle. Instantly, I knew what I needed to do. I needed Nichelle to see this; I needed her to see the church as it is, not as I made it out to be.

The church is a group of people who are all on their God journey. Some are further than others, some are seeking, some are observing, some are committed, and most are hurting. They all need Jesus and some kind of healing in their lives, but at this very moment all of them were standing together for one purpose–my little girl's healing.

The next service, I picked her up from her class early, and we walked in the back doors and stood where she could have the best view of the church.

I held her in my arms as our pastor told this room full of people about the battle Nichelle was fighting. The pastor put his hand on James' shoulder and began to pray. The entire room bowed their head in unison and stood in agreement with the prayer. I whispered in my little girl's ear, "They are praying for you; every single person in here believes that God will heal you." Her face lit up with surprise and with the biggest smile on her face she asked, "They are praying for me?" With pride in my voice, I said, "Yes, baby girl they are praying for you."

That is the day offense was silenced.

The church will never get everything right. It will always be messy, offend, and often make mistakes, because the church is not a building–the church is the people. We are the people that make up the church, and we don't always get everything right. We are messy and are bound to offend someone. We are human and we make mistakes.

We are also strong. We are an army of men and women with the same purpose, united with one singular mission: to change the world for Jesus. We need to silence the voice of offense. We need to stop seeing the church as the enemy. As more women balance on the three-legged stool of family, faith, and career, the need to silence the voice of offense is more important than ever. As offense grows in your heart and mind, the leg of faith gets weak. If that leg is weak, you will come crashing down, and you will take your world and your purpose with you. You will take them down to a bow.

I see this happening with more frequency by single moms, married moms, single ladies, married ladies, divorced moms, divorced ladies, widowed moms, and widowed ladies. Ladies offended that their trouble and struggles are not addressed in one hour one day a week. They are offended that their gifts, talents, calling, and purpose are not recognized. Offended that they are not seen and heard.

The church can't be expected to answer all your questions, speak to your unique situation, or share infinite wisdom; the church is comprised of people, limited in answers, limited to their experiences, and limited to one hour on Sunday. However, God is available 24/7. He is all-knowing, possessing all the answers, willing and waiting to share them with you.

"If you need wisdom, ask our generous God,
and he will give it to you.
He will not rebuke you for asking. But when you ask him,
be sure that your faith is in God alone.
Do not waver, for a person with divided loyalty is
as unsettled as a wave of the sea that is
blown and tossed by the wind."
JAMES 1:5-6 NLT

God will share his wisdom with you generously, but your faith must be in God alone. We can address every trouble and struggle in our lives with the Word of God and in prayer. The answers, encouragement, help, hope, and support are all at our fingertips. It is easier to be offended, and it is easier to silence the solutions we have available than to put effort into finding them. I didn't want answers; I wanted to be mad. I didn't want to seek Jesus; I wanted him brought to me. I wanted it to happen my way. I was wrong.

We are wrong to want church done our way, and we are only right when we silence offense and see Jesus and the church for who they are.

Offense will always make you bow, leaving you focused on yourself. When standing up to offense, you have a view of Jesus, a view of the solutions, and a view of the people around you who need you to share Jesus with them.

If we are to share Jesus, we must know who he is. If we are to share his hope, we have to know where to find it. If we are to share his love, we must know how to give it. If we are to change the world for Jesus, we can't rely on being taught about him; we must seek him for ourselves, and we must know him on an intimate level.

It was the privilege of a lifetime to hold my little girl in the back of the auditorium and show her the church as it is meant to be seen. No longer offended, I looked on at the praying church with pride and gratitude for the freedom and privilege to be a part of it.

A few years later, James was invited to speak to the staff of a church. He shared Nichelle's story with them and talked a little bit about her condition. Spontaneously he asked the question, "Has anyone ever heard of NF?" One hand in the back of the room went up, and I was surprised. The only reason a person would know about this condition is if someone in their life has it.

When it was over, the gentleman who raised his hand came up to us and told us that his wife had NF. He said, "I would love for your daughter and my wife to meet sometime." Not too long after that day, Nichelle and I ran into his wife. She looked at Nichelle and said, "I have NF too," and they high-fived then proceeded to share their stories and experiences—they were laughing like two old friends. I watched as this married, mother of two and my 8-year-old daughter talked, and I was moved by the way God's hand has been on my little girl's life. She was confident, unafraid, and unmoved by her health issues. She had a foundation of faith laid by watching a church come together and model it for her. She saw the church as it was meant to be seen and she modeled it.

They finished up their conversation, and Nichelle went off to play. The lady looked at me, and with tears running down her face, said, "I have never laughed or smiled while talking about my NF before. I am grateful for your daughter and her courage because it gives me courage."

What we let into our hearts we will give to the world. If we let offense in, we will give offense to the world. If we let encouragement in, we will take encouragement to the world. If we allow God to change us, we will bring that same change into our world.

Nichelle has never been ashamed of her faith in Jesus. She is a church-inviting machine, an unashamed champion of the message of Jesus. She loves the church and loves bringing her friends to church. We frequently have to make multiple trips picking up and dropping kids off at church, because my daughter got to see the church as it should be seen. She is a pastor's daughter, so she has seen the church at its worst, but she has also seen it at its best. She chooses to silence offense, and she chooses to become an effective part of the army.

We can choose offense, or we can choose to silence it. We can choose to become the obstacle that keeps the beautiful message of Jesus from being shared with the world, or we can be the army who removes the obstacle of offense and bravely, boldly, and confidently stands up for Jesus and steps into our purpose and calling.

Each one of us equipped and purposed to change the world for Jesus, and each one of us is a crucial part of the church.

"In his grace, God has given us different gifts
for doing certain things well.

So if God has given you the ability to prophesy, speak out with as much faith as God has given you. If your gift is serving others, serve them well. If you are a teacher, teach well. If your gift is to encourage others, be encouraging. If it is giving, give generously.

If God has given you leadership ability, take the responsibility seriously.

And if you have a gift for showing kindness to others, do it gladly.

Don't just pretend to love others. Really love them. Hate what is wrong. Hold tightly to what is good. Love each other with genuine affection, and take delight in honoring each other. Never be lazy, but work hard and serve the Lord enthusiastically.

Rejoice in our confident hope. Be patient in trouble,
and keep on praying.
When God's people are in need, be ready to help them."
ROMANS 12:6-13 NLT

The enemy would love nothing more than to see the church destroy itself from the inside out. He would love for women to be offended and silenced. He would love for you to think that your purpose can only be lived out within the walls of the church building. He would love for you to believe that the only way to fulfill your purpose is through the volunteer positions that are offered. He would love to see you limited by rules and tradition.

There are no limits with God. There are no walls, no traditions. There is only obedience and submission, calling and purpose, and the mandate to not just serve in the church, but to also leave the walls of the church and GO into all the world and preach, share, and spread the good news of Jesus.

"And then he told them,
'Go into all the world and preach the Good News to everyone.'"
MARK 16:15 NLT

We, the women of the church, are created on purpose and for a purpose. We were created to change the world for Jesus by being the church and created to step into our purpose and take the message of Jesus into a lost and broken world. We were chosen to love the church, to be the church, and to leave the walls of the church, taking our God-given purpose and giving it freely to a world that needs it.

When you choose to no longer be silenced by offense, but instead choose to stand in the face of it, you are not alone. God is standing right beside you. He stands next to you and says, "Now this is a girl I can change the world through."

8 SILENCED BY PRIDE

We, the Christian women of this world, are a silenced army. Silenced by pride.

Pride: the downfall of nations, corporations, relationships, marriages, the church, and God's army.
Pride steals our joy, contentment, self-esteem, confidence, hope, peace, and unity.
Pride keeps us comparing and competing, selfish and self-centered, and miserable and lonely. Pride thinly veils our fears, vulnerabilities, shame, inadequacies, and insecurities.

Desperate to hide our faults from the world, we build a tight wall around ourselves leaving no room for anyone else. We wall family and friends out, we wall accountability out, we wall our fellow Christ-follower out, and we wall God out.

We bow to pride, and we choose silence.

Our world needs all of us in the battle, and our world needs all of our purposes to come together to work as the army of God.

If we are constantly comparing ourselves to each other and rendering ourselves less than, we sneak the poison of pride into the troops. The voice of pride will rise up and instead of being confident in who God created us to be, we tear each other down to a level that makes ourselves feel better than or make ourselves feel superior. And the cycle continues, until the poison has spread through the ranks. An army brought down to a bow by pride.

God and pride cannot occupy the same space, so where there is pride, there is no God. If God and pride were in the same space, God would outshine it–pride won't let that happen. Pride says I know better than God, that I am better than God.

"In his pride the wicked man does not seek him;
in all his thoughts there is no room for God."
PSALM 10:4 NIV

Pride sneaks in when we are uncertain about who we are in Christ, and when we don't believe what he says about us to be true. He says we are masterpieces; we were created on purpose and with a purpose. He says we were created to change the world for him.

All too often, we believe the lie being fed to us by the enemy: The lie that says we are not equal in God's eyes, and that we are better than some and worse than others.

God's truth is this: We are all loved equally and are treasured, and we were created with the purpose to change the world for Jesus. Each of us is unique and different on purpose, chosen for different assignments, with none more important than the other.

We complicate this simple message with pride; we look at the people around us and rank each other. We compare our lives with theirs. We compare our looks, weight, and fashion; we compare our friends, boyfriends, husbands and kids; we compare our calling and purpose. As a result, we are left unsatisfied.

This lack of satisfaction and contentment with who God made us leads to pride and anger; these emotions compel us to action—pride. Pride will push us to be better than or to make others less than. Women of the world are silencing each other because of pride.

Not one of us is immune to the pride we often succumb to, like the trap of social media, the spark that ignites pride in many of us. We scroll through snapshots of people's lives, and we compare the entirety of our lives to their snapshot. Unsatisfied with the comparison, we criticize each other for not "being real," authentic, or transparent. We come to the conclusion that their "real" can't be real, because if it is, our "real" is not good enough.

Comparison is the thief of joy and contentment—the key that unlocks the door to pride.

Instead of cheering each other on and supporting and encouraging each other, we fight each other in a silent pride war.

The enemy watches, loving every minute of it. He knows that if we are fighting each other, we won't focus on fighting him, and we won't change the world for Jesus. All he has to do is sit back and wait for the fall and our self-imposed destruction.

"Pride goes before destruction, a haughty spirit before a fall."
PROVERBS 16:18 NIV

Pride brings destruction to our relationship with God, each other, and the purpose we are supposed to fulfill. It leaves us lost in a maze of discontentment, searching for a way out but finding none.

"As Jesus and the disciples continued on their way to Jerusalem, they came to a certain village where a woman named Martha welcomed him into her home.

Her sister, Mary, sat at the Lord's feet, listening to what he taught.
But Martha was distracted by the big dinner she was preparing.
She came to Jesus and said, 'Lord, doesn't it seem unfair to you
that my sister just sits here while I do all the work?
Tell her to come and help me.'
But the Lord said to her,
'My dear Martha, you are worried and upset over all these details!
There is only one thing worth being concerned about.
Mary has discovered it,
and it will not be taken away from her.'"

LUKE 10:38-42 NLT

This story has a way of making us choose a side. Some of us are all about team Martha, because it makes sense that in a room full of men it would be her responsibility to take on the traditional and expected gender role of preparing the meal. I have a feeling that for Martha it was about more than the traditional role she was fulfilling; I think this was a pleasure for her. She was all about making everyone feel welcomed and comfortable. She wasn't preparing appetizers or desserts or a snack, the scriptures say—she was preparing a big dinner. She was going above and beyond for Jesus and the other guests. This was what she was purposed to do and what she loved to do.

Others of us are thinking team Mary, totally team Mary! Because Mary wasn't restrained by tradition, she sat where the men sat. She didn't stand against the wall in the back, she didn't blend in with the crowd, and she didn't bow to tradition or society. Mary shirked her expected role and sat where she wanted to be—where she needed to be—at the feet of Jesus, not where she was expected to be.

There are theologies and whole denominations that have chosen the Mary or Martha team. There are those who think Martha, "the hostess with the mostest," behaved properly and honorably. Then there are those who believe Mary was just as much in her role and element as Martha was.

Most of the time we will choose the side we most identify with or are comfortable with. But why do we choose a team at all? Why do we want Mary and Martha to be doing the same thing or living the same purpose? Why do we think one is right over the other? Pride. Pride in thinking we know better than anyone else. Pride in thinking we know better than God.

I don't like to cook. I do cook, but I don't enjoy it. My mom loves to cook and is so very good at it. She is one of those, whip something fantastic up from nothing, kind of cooks. She always makes fresh, homemade food, and if you look in her freezer you will only find frozen meats like chicken, fish, and turkey. You will never find microwaveable foods in her refrigerator. She is amazing. My mom is and always will be "the hostess with the mostest," and she does it effortlessly. She does it so perfectly that I felt self-imposed pressure to do it the same way. I used to feel that if I wasn't as good as she is then I was somehow less than. My mom never made me feel this way; in fact, she is one of my biggest fans and supporters. But for some unknown reason I had to beat her, be her, compete with her to be enough. One day, she told me how proud of me she was. She told me she admired my strength and wished she had some of my strength years ago when she needed it. This blew me away, because I was trying to be her while she was wanting what I had. We get along so well because of our differences; she is so strong in areas I am weak and I have strength in areas she doesn't think she has it. God created us on purpose, with the strengths we have, the purposes we have, the voices we have, and the abilities we have. He didn't make a mistake by making us different–it is a part of his perfect plan.

Mary didn't have the problem of pride or comparison. She boldly sat in her seat at the feet of Jesus and had zero guilt over shirking her duties as hostess. She was determined to learn and grow from Jesus' teachings.

Martha, on the other hand, had a big problem with it. She took her responsibilities as hostess seriously, and she expected Mary to do the same. So much so, that she wasn't going to be satisfied until Jesus corrected

Mary. She wasn't content with scolding Mary later in private or trying to understand how important sitting at the feet of Jesus was to Mary. Martha was determined to have Mary corrected, and in the most public way in front of their guests. She asked Jesus to correct, fix, scold, or rebuke her sister. Martha truly believed she was right in her request; she believed Mary needed to be put back on the right path, back in her rightful, traditional, and expected place.

Pride will always want us to lead people to the place we are, to the place that makes sense for us, to the place that doesn't push us out of our comfort zone. We will choose comfort for everyone around us, and we will choose each other's purpose based on what we are comfortable watching. We either want to push each other into the "kitchen" or out of the "kitchen" without any thought as to where God wants them, only to where we want them.

Knowing someone who pushes the norms, steps outside of traditional roles, or blazes new trails makes us uncomfortable. Instead of encouraging, praying for, or cheering them on as they pursue their God-given purpose, we withdraw from them, refuse to support them, and most often than not, a posse is formed to stop them. We talk behind their back, we refuse to listen to them, we do our best to discredit them, and we actively silence them.

We are not a victim of pride: We are volunteers.

If Jesus were here today, I think his response to our need to push each other into traditional norms, positions, and titles would be the exact same response he gave to Martha. "My dear Martha, you are worried and upset over all these details! There is only one thing worth being concerned about. Mary has discovered it, and it will not be taken away from her."

I love that Jesus addresses Martha with so much kindness, patience, and love. He never corrected her for serving in her role as hostess, and he never corrected her for not sitting at his feet. His only response was to help her understand that Mary had found her place at the feet of Jesus, even if it wasn't the traditional role that Jesus, Martha, and Mary were accustomed to, and she was where she was purposed to be.

Jesus didn't scold Mary either. With anyone and everyone else, her actions would have been unacceptable, but not with Jesus. I am struck by the fact that the only person upset with Mary was Martha–her sister and friend. No one else had a problem with Mary's decision to sit at the feet of Jesus. Martha, who should have supported her sister, was her biggest critic. This close relationship made it easy for Martha to overlook Mary's heart for Jesus. Jesus was pleased with Mary and made it possible for every woman after her to sit at his feet and boldly step into our purpose. Jesus made it possible to not be silenced by pressure, pride, jealousy, or lack of understanding from the people around us, but to courageously step out of tradition and into the life God purposed us to live.

Jesus was patient with both Mary and Martha, because he knew that we are all purposed to be, do, accomplish and fulfill something different, just as he planned. Jesus' loving and patient response was what both women needed, and it is what we need even today. Jesus said, "Mary has discovered it, and it will not be taken away from her."

What is "it"? "It" is what we are purposed to do, and "it" can never be taken away from us. "It" is Jesus; "it" always circles back to Jesus.

We were created on purpose, and we were created with a purpose. We were created to change the world for Jesus. Mary's "it" was to sit at the feet of Jesus, Martha's "it" was to serve him, and your "it" is to live your purpose without comparison or pride. Your "it" is to change the world for Jesus in whatever way he has created you to do it.

There is no reason for pride or comparison in our ranks. There is only a need for every single one of us to step into our purpose and fulfill it if we are going to change the world for Jesus.

"In his grace, God has given us different gifts
for doing certain things well.
So if God has given you the ability to prophesy,
speak out with as much faith as God has given you.
If your gift is serving others, serve them well.

If you are a teacher, teach well.
If your gift is to encourage others, be encouraging.
If it is giving, give generously.
If God has given you leadership ability, take the responsibility seriously.
and if you have a gift for showing kindness to others, do it gladly."
ROMANS 12:6-8 NLT

The world will not be changed by conformity but by our differences.

The world will not be changed by complacency but by determination.

The world will not be changed by pride in ourselves but pride in God.

We silence pride by focusing on our own purpose while simultaneously cheering on our fellow Christ-followers on their journey to live out their purpose and calling.

"Do nothing out of selfish ambition or empty pride,
but in humility consider others more important than yourselves.
Each of you should look not only to your own interests,
but also to the interests of others."
PHILIPPIANS 2:3-4 BSB

This scripture doesn't say your life, purpose or calling shouldn't be seen as important; it means we should see our life and purpose as part of God's greater plan, not that our plan needs to become God's plan. God is asking us to stay humble, know our place and purpose, and to help further his plan by partnering and encouraging others as they fulfill their purpose in whatever capacity God has purposed them to do it.

The impact your God-given purpose will make is far more important than worrying about how your purpose or the purpose of the people around you will impact you.

Your purpose may not be showcased on the world stage. It may not look good on social media, and it may not ever be seen by anyone other than you and the people who are changed because of it. However, that doesn't mean it is less than, less important, less impactful, or less inspiring. It means you have found "it" and "it" will never be taken from you. It means you are changing the world for Jesus. It means you are not a victim of pride but a volunteer to change it.

The day I wrote this chapter, I took a break to discuss the findings of the consultant we contacted to give us advice about the effectiveness of our ministry on both social media and our website. We asked how we could improve; we were seeking answers so we could better equip and partner with men and women around the world who want to join the movement of changing the world for Jesus.

About two minutes into the honest and requested feedback, I started to feel defensive. Pride began to swell up in my heart. I immediately recognized pride in my thoughts (since I was just writing about it minutes before) but chose not to silence pride–instead going into defensive mode. While my husband was filling me in on the consultant's expert opinion, I was sitting there silently defending every decision I made and every bit of content I had ever written. Even the stuff that I knew needed to be changed, I was defending. God mercifully broke into my thoughts and said, "Your pride will kill this ministry." That was exactly what I needed to hear, and it shook me to my core. I instantly knew why the enemy is a fan of tempting us with pride. Pride kills dreams, hopes, honesty, transparency, intimacy, partnerships, good intentions, well-laid-out plans, purpose, and calling.

In the moments when pride had me bowing to it, I wasn't thinking about everyone who would be inspired, encouraged, motivated, and challenged to change the world for Jesus. I was thinking about myself and how it felt to have every aspect of my ministry critiqued, every decision questioned, and every dream challenged.

I was more concerned about my feelings than I was about my impact.

The consultant was doing his job. He wasn't trying to insult me; he was trying to help me reach further, soar higher, impact more people, and get better results. He wasn't speaking with pride; he was talking from experience and as an expert in his field.

My responsibility was to think of the impact on the world I will make rather than the impact change will have on me.

Pride made change the enemy rather than an ally. Pride tempted me to turn away sound advice for the sake of my feelings. Pride would have brought a ministry that impacts people around the globe down to a bow. I silenced pride and listened with the future impact of my ministry in mind. I got excited, and now I can't wait to make changes, grow, and be stretched. I can't wait to see what God does with a ministry unimpeded by pride.

Silencing pride gave me an opportunity to listen, learn, and grow. The process of iron sharpening iron is not comfortable. Sparks will fly, but after it's all said and done, we will be a sharpened tool willing and ready to change the world for Jesus—fueled by a fire in our souls set by the sparks of iron sharpening iron.

"As iron sharpens iron, so one person sharpens another."
PROVERBS 27:17 NIV

We, the Christian women of this world, no longer a silenced army. We are an army silencing pride. We are confident about who we are in Christ, and we believe what he says about us is true. We are masterpieces, created on purpose and with a purpose. We were created to change the world for Jesus. We are united in our cause of bringing unity and encouragement to each other, furthering God's plan and fulfilling it.

We listen to each other, learn from each other, and grow together. We are not prideful, selfish, or self-centered. We no longer compare our lives or calling, and we no longer compete for importance. We cheer each other on, stand up for each other, and trust God's purpose and calling for each other's lives is good. We are a humble army, thinking of each other before ourselves and understanding that we are better and stronger together. We are ready to change the world for Jesus.

"Two people are better off than one, for they can help each other succeed."

ECCLESIASTES 4:9 NLT

We are more than two: We are millions helping each other succeed in our mission to share Jesus with a lost and dying world.

When you choose to no longer be silenced by pride, but instead choose to stand in the face of it, you are not alone. God is standing right beside you. He stands next to you and says, "Now this is a girl I can change the world through."

9 SILENCED BY CULTURE

We, the Christian women of this world, are a silenced army. Silenced by culture.

Culture that says you are wrong. Culture that says God is wrong. A silenced Army. Silenced by culture.

We cast our vote when we stay silent, and we give our approval with our lack of action. We are changing the world by remaining silent. We are making a difference by not making one at all.

Silenced by the pressures of this world. Silenced by the voice in our head. Silenced willingly.

Pressured to fit in.
Pressured to believe that wrong is right.
Pressured to accept lies as truth.
Pressured to believe that the message of Jesus breeds hate.
Pressured to water down our beliefs.
Pressured to hide our faith.
Pressured to believe God is wrong.
Pressured to bow to culture.
Pressured to stay silent.

Satan, the thief of our voice, the killer of our courage, and the destroyer of our faith has proven to be a worthy adversary. He has gathered his army, given them a voice, whispered lies, created a cause, and silenced his opposers.

We, the Christian women, stay silent—seemingly unaffected by the battle, hiding in our homes and churches, ignoring the voice insulting our faith, our beliefs, and our God. We tell ourselves, *As long as it doesn't affect me, it's not my battle to fight.* We bury our heads in the sand, waiting for the change we are supposed to bring. Waiting for someone else to fight our battle.

Our enemy is not out to steal, kill, and destroy your way of life; he is out to destroy God's way of life. The life God set in motion and has planned for us—along with the morals he put in place and the guardrails he set up. The enemy is out to destroy the purpose God created each one of us with.

When we accepted Jesus, we volunteered for the army of Christ and agreed to fight for and uphold the Word of God. If our enemy can destroy God's way of life, our way of life will follow.

Silently, we bow to culture. We compromise what we believe in the name of grace. We agree to sin to keep the peace, and we turn a blind eye to fit in. We take absolute truth and redefine it to fit our own desires. Finding it easier to bow than to stand, we are silenced. We conform to culture's distorted view of truth.

"Don't copy the behavior and customs of this world,
but let God transform you
into a new person by changing the way you think."
ROMANS 12:2a NLT

As women in the army of Christ, we don't get to interpret the Bible as we see fit; we don't get to pick and choose which parts we will follow and which ones we won't.

We have to fight the pressures to be convinced by culture to accept things as right that God says are wrong.

We don't get to contradict God. We don't define sin, God does. We don't get to rewrite the Bible to fit the culture around us. Anything that opposes or is in contradiction to the Word of God is a lie. Jesus says this about the enemy in John 8:44b NLT; *"...When he lies, it is consistent with his character; for he is a liar and the father of lies."* His lies have deceived us from the very beginning, starting with Eve, but it doesn't have to continue. We don't have to believe them, and we don't have to give in to them.

We are not victims of culture: We are volunteers to change it.

We were created on purpose and with a purpose. We were created to change the world for Jesus, not to hide from it. We are to be transformed to be like Jesus. To be like Jesus is to allow him to change the way we think, change the way we listen, and change the way we see the world around us. To be transformed by Jesus is to discern God's truths from Satan's lies. To be transformed is to see the world as God sees it–a world that needs Jesus.

In 1 Samuel chapter 17, we read about Goliath, the Israelite army, and David.

Goliath the Philistine–a giant in stature and in intimidation–and an opposer of Israel and their God. He taunted God's army: a silent army. He yelled insults at them for 40 days and nights, with the arrogance of an unopposed bully. His message was "I defy the armies of Israel today!" What he really meant was, "I defy your God."

The Army of soldiers, ready and armed for battle–chosen and trained to defend and protect the people of God–were silenced by the size of the giant and the volume of his voice. An army brought down to a bow by words and threats; they were "terrified and deeply shaken." Their only defense for silence was a question: "Have you seen the giant?"

David was a boy, a shepherd. He was small in stature, unequipped for battle, untrained, and unarmed. He was unafraid by the size of the giant, the volume of his voice, or the daily taunts. He responded to the insults and taunts with bravery, boldness, and courage: "Don't worry about this Philistine, I'll go fight him!"

The only response to David's courage from a bowed army was discouragement.

The silenced, speaking up only to silence the unafraid, bold, and courageous.

"Don't be ridiculous!" Saul replied. "There's no way you can fight this Philistine and possibly win! You're only a boy, and he's been a man of war since his youth."

David, unmoved by discouragement or the size of the giant, bravely stands when the rest of the army bows. He boldly and courageously walked onto the battlefield, alone. He can feel all eyes on him; he knows they are waiting for him to fail.

They have very little faith in him, but even less in themselves, so they let him stand alone.

The army's fate lies in the hands of this one brave, untrained, and unequipped boy. They know if David loses, they all become slaves to the enemy; still, they silently bow to the giant.

But David wasn't concerned about the size of the giant; he knew the size of his God, and there was no comparison. He would not allow this giant to mock his God.

David replied to the Philistine, "You come to me with sword, spear, and javelin, but I come to you in the name of the LORD of Heaven's Armies–the God of the armies of Israel, whom you have defied. And everyone assembled here will know that the LORD rescues his people, but not with sword and spear. This is the LORD's battle, and he will give you to us!"

David, alone in his conviction and courage, was willing to stand up to the giant with no earthly guarantee that he would win. He silenced the giant the moment he stood up and stepped onto the battlefield. His victory was believing that God was on his side. His motivation was to defend his God, who will not be mocked. David stood on the battlefield, facing a giant and his army, and behind David, an army unwilling to fight, silenced and bowing.

David leaned down to pick up his only earthly defense—five smooth stones. When he stood, he did not stand alone; he stood with God.

As he stood, this boy cast a God-sized shadow.

The giant is silenced.

Culture: The unopposed giant who hurls insults and taunts God's silent army, the church. Big, intimidating, loud, armed, battle-tested, unafraid, and repetitious in its insults to our God. It is unafraid to invite us into a battle, unafraid to mock our God, unafraid to challenge our beliefs, and unafraid to provoke us onto the battlefield.

Unafraid because it knows we are afraid.

The silent army: the Christian women of the church. The silent and afraid, the voice of discouragement to those who bravely choose to stand when the army bows. They watch as she bravely faces the giant. But instead of cheers, encouragement, and support, there is silence. They have very little faith in her, but even less in themselves, so they let her stand alone. They know if she loses, they all become slaves, yet still they silently bow to culture.

The Christian women of the church: the silencer of culture. Alone in our convictions and courage, we are willing to stand up to the giant, with no earthly guarantee that we will win. We silence the giant the moment we stand up and step onto the battlefield. Our victory is believing that God is on our side. Our motivation is to defend our God, who will not be mocked. Together we stand on the battlefield, facing a giant and his army, and behind us, God.

We bravely, courageously, and boldly stand, but we don't stand alone; we stand with God, casting a God-sized shadow.

The giant is silenced.

When you choose to silence the giant (the voice of culture) you will never feel as small as you are. When you stand, God is standing with you—and the shadow you cast is God-sized.

We were made on purpose and with a purpose.

We were made to change the world for Jesus.

Silenced no more, we stand up to culture. We are uncompromising, unmoved, and unashamed in what we believe and in whom we believe in; we unapologetically speak the truth of Jesus in love. We look for opportunities to change the world and culture.

"For we are not fighting against flesh-and-blood enemies,
but against evil rulers and authorities of the unseen world,
against mighty powers in this dark world,
and against evil spirits in the heavenly places."
EPHESIANS 6:12 NLT

Culture: a way of life for some, a widely accepted belief by most. A forced perspective by the vocal few, followed by the masses. Culture gathers a following of billions—too many in the following to know that their leader is lost and leading them to death, so they blindly follow the culture. Wanting to fit in and not be left out, God's army follows; we join the masses, all while knowing it leads to death, destruction, hurt, compromised faith, and distorted view of God's truths. We think we can keep our faith in tact while following the faithless. We cannot save the world with the good news of Jesus if we are joining them on the road to destruction.

"God sent his Son into the world not to judge the world, but to save the world through him."

JOHN 3:17 NLT

No longer a silenced army, we step onto the battlefield–not to fight with lost people but to fight for them. Our weapons are meant to destroy the lies of culture and bring life to people. We fight with the message of Jesus, and this message will replace lies with truth, bring hope to the hopeless, healing to the sick and broken, joy to the depressed, peace to the anxious, direction to the lost, significance to the unseen, a hearing ear to the unheard, and Heaven to the hellbound.

Too many people are caught in the grips of culture and are too afraid to leave for fear they will stand alone. They believe to be a part of the world is to be a part of something big and greater than themselves. They so badly want to be a part of it and be accepted; they don't want to be set apart, rejected by culture, and hated.

"The world would love you as one of its own if you belonged to it, but you are no longer part of the world. I chose you to come out of the world, so it hates you."

JOHN 15:19 NLT

We, the Christian army of the world, are no longer silenced. We offer refuge, hope, love, peace, forgiveness, and freedom through Jesus. This message, locked away for far too long, is now spreading like wildfire by the unafraid, unashamed, and the standing. We, the women of the church and God's army, are not rejected but accepted by God–joining an army with others just like us, bringing light to darkness, a way out of culture's grip, a path to life, and an eternity with Jesus.

The message of Jesus spread by those casting a God-sized shadow.

She walked into the nail salon looking tired, broken, and defeated. She silently sat next to me without looking at me. I did my best to avoid making eye contact, because I was also tired and looking forward to a few minutes of quiet.

Her phone begins to vibrate. She answers, responds quickly, and then hangs up. She then starts talking to me as if she was resuming a conversation we were previously having. "My son's favorite color is red." Unsure how to respond, I said, "I like the color red too." She replies, "His funeral is tomorrow, and I'm going to wear red on my nails in honor of him. Do you think this is a pretty shade of red?" I felt like she was asking me if her son would approve of that particular shade of red. I had no way of knowing which shade of red her son liked, but I did know she needed to hear that she was honoring her son in every possible way she could. I quickly respond with, "I think he would love it."

She went on to tell me the story of how her 9-year-old son was killed in a boating accident a week earlier, and the driver of the boat that hit them was drunk and walked away unharmed. Her son was sitting on her lap when they were hit and was instantly killed while she was thrown from the boat.

I lifted my head and, for the first time, really looked at her. She had a huge knot on her forehead. She was bruised and had noticeable deep cuts. I can imagine that her heart felt far worse.

She shared that her son died while she was unconscious. Her first words when she woke up in the hospital were questions about her son. "Is he okay? Is he here? Can I see him?" She told the story without a single tear, while I struggled to hold mine back. My heart was hurting, and I was feeling everything she was suppressing. I instantly knew she needed Jesus–the only way she was going to get through this was with Jesus.

She trailed off from her story without telling me the ending; I could see she was lost in the memory of that day and every day since. The silence was deafening, and everyone in the salon was listening as she told her story, then silently trailed off. Each of us pictured ourselves in this tragedy and wondered how she was sitting there so calm and collected.

My compassion for this stranger was overwhelming. I wanted to do something to ease her pain, but what could I say ... what could I do? I couldn't bring back her son, I couldn't go back in time and save them from this disaster, and I couldn't take her pain away. All that was left to do was share Jesus with her.

I was minutes away from my nails being done, and I knew I had to pray with this grieving mother. All eyes and ears were focused on the two of us, and for a moment, it silenced me. Every silencer the enemy could muster up was flowing through my mind, like a giant yelling his taunts to drown out the voice of God. Then a clear voice told me to silence the giant and stand up—stand up to the giant, stand up for this grieving mother, stand up for those watching and listening, and stand up for me.

Not once did she give me any indication that she believed in Jesus or had hope—the kind of hope that only Christians have when tragedy strikes. I heard the voice again, telling me to silence the giant and stand up.

Giving myself no time to bow to the pressure of fear or culture, I asked her, "Can I pray with you?" With a sigh she said, "Yes, please." It was as if she was just waiting for hope, waiting for the strength she knew she would receive from a caring stranger who prayed.

We held hands, and I prayed a prayer that I would want to hear If I had just lost my own son. I prayed a prayer that introduced Jesus to an audience of spectators listening in and watching. I silenced every voice that said, "You're in public, people will stare, people will think you're crazy, and people will judge you." That silence left room for the voice of God to give me courage and for God to provide me with the words to pray.

I finished praying and looked up at her; the tears she had been holding back were now flowing down her cheeks. I wanted to do so much more for her, but I knew I was there for one reason and that reason was to show her Jesus.

My family says I have the words "talk to me" written on my forehead, because everywhere we go people tell me their story. Maybe they are right, but I think they see Jesus in me. I think they see the hope that culture can't offer them, and they want the peace that conforming can't bring them. They see answers they have been searching for, and they see truth amongst the lies. They don't see perfection; they see that a process is happening and, whatever it is, they want it.

We were created on purpose and with a purpose. We were created to change the world for Jesus–to stand up when there is pressure to bow, pray when there is pressure to stay silent, and offer Jesus when there is pressure to keep him to ourselves.

This is a dangerous message to the enemy. His tricks to silence us are being revealed; his plan is failing, because we will not be silenced. We will not bow; we will change the world, and we will silence culture.

The battle is real, and it is raging around us. It is crucial to Satan's plan to silence every ONE of us. He knows he isn't as effective as we are at discouraging each other, pulling each other down, demotivating each other, and silencing each other. He's hoping the silenced will bring the standing to a bow, because he needs every ONE of us to be silenced for his plan to work.

He only has to silence one of us to silence the rest, for if one of us speaks up, it gives courage to the rest.

The battle is real, and you are needed in it. Every ONE of us is crucial to the plan God has. We must encourage each other, push each other, and motivate each other. We must sharpen each other. Every ONE–including you–the ONE is needed for God's plan to be fulfilled.

"Be on guard. Stand firm in the faith. Be courageous. Be strong."

1 CORINTHIANS 16:13 NLT

Women of Christ stand firm in your faith. Be courageous! Be strong!

Stand up unafraid to stand out.
Silence culture.
Unapologetically believe.
Stand up and say, wrong is wrong and right is right.
Believe truth over lies.
Boldly proclaim that the message of Jesus breeds love and not hate.
Be strong in your beliefs.
Be confident in your faith.
Believe God is right.
Bravely stand up to culture.
Be silent no more.

Jesus, the giver of your voice, the reason for your courage, and the foundation of your faith has proven to be a worthy Savior. He has gathered his army, given you a voice, and created a cause. He's changing the world through you. It won't be easy; you won't always love the process of fulfilling your purpose and the calling on your life. The message of Jesus will not be embraced by everyone you tell, and you won't always be understood or accepted. However, our job is not to enforce the message of Jesus—our purpose is to share it. Emboldened by the God-sized shadow we cast, we don't back down, we don't give up, we don't silence our voice, and we don't bow.

"I have told you all this so that you may have peace in me.
Here on earth you will have many trials and sorrows.
But take heart,
because I have overcome the world."
JOHN 16:33 NLT

When you choose to no longer be silenced by culture, but instead choose to stand in the face of it, you are not alone. God is standing right beside you. He stands next to you and says, "Now this is a girl I can change the world through."

10 SILENCED BY DISTRACTION

We, the Christian women of this world, are a silenced army. Silenced by distraction.

Distraction is a sly weapon used by the enemy. Distraction keeps us focused on good and bad things so we will miss the God things in our lives.

Distraction will keep us following whatever life throws at us, and distraction makes everything in our lives except God urgent. Distraction has a snowball effect, and if you open the door to it, distraction can take your whole life with it, one day at a time.

A distraction: keeping up, getting ahead, fitting in, chasing dreams, building a life, climbing the ladder, shattering ceilings, and holding on for dear life to everything you want over everything God wants for you and to do through you.

"I am saying this for your benefit,
not to place restrictions on you.

I want you to do whatever will help you serve the Lord best,
with as few distractions as possible."
1 CORINTHIANS 7:35 NLT

We are not victims of distraction: We are volunteers. Distraction will hold our attention for as long as we are willing to let it. Distraction is a choice.

The first year my kids attended school online was tough. We had to discipline ourselves to stay focused. I say ourselves because I was right there with them during school, and I was just as easily distracted as they were.

We would start our day strong, fizzle a bit before lunch, come back from lunch wired, and then fizzle again around midday. After a few months, we figured out what worked for us and things were going smoothly. For some reason though, our school days were getting longer and longer, and I couldn't figure out why.

My kids, being the brilliant people that they are, learned how to distract me. They knew if one of them started singing that I would join in. They knew if there was a bird out the window and they pointed it out to me, I would encourage everyone to get up to look at the bird. They knew which topics would keep me talking and would distract me from the project we were working on. My precious little angels were playing me like a fiddle.

It wasn't until they were having to do school work well into the evening that they realized that distracting mom (so they didn't have to do their work) was only hurting them.

I'll let you in on a little secret. I figured out what my littles were doing early on, but I let it play out. I knew if I was always telling them about the consequences of distraction, they wouldn't believe me. They would think I was taking their fun away or being too hard on them, so I let them feel the pain of distraction so they would stop searching for it.

Changing the world for Jesus is hard work: It takes discipline. It will require us to silence distraction. We are reaping the consequences of distraction from generations before us who were unwilling to do the hard work, but instead found relief and solace in distraction.

Women, the army of God, no longer has the luxury of time to be distracted. We can no longer succumb to it or search for it. The world needs every single one of us focused, disciplined, and ready to change the world for Jesus. Our time on this earth is short, but our impact will last for generations. If we want to pass on hope past our lifetime, we will have to set aside the distractions of this world and put into focus the importance of living our lives on purpose.

"So, then, be careful how you live. Do not be unwise but wise, making the best use of your time because the times are evil."

EPHESIANS 5:15-16 ISV

"Make the best use of your time," means we have to take time seriously–it is finite while we are on this earth. Each minute that passes is a minute spent, a minute invested, or a minute wasted. We choose how to spend our time, and once spent, we can never get it back. Time can be full of purpose and impact or it can be wasted and squandered. What is the best use of your time? What gets all of your focus and attention? Are you living on purpose or chasing the distractions the enemy throws on your path? How you spend your time and your life pursuits is your choice, but distraction cannot dictate how you spend your life–it can only tempt you to follow it.

"But all too quickly the message is crowded out by the worries of this life, the lure of wealth, and the desire for other things, so no fruit is produced."

MARK 4:19 NLT

Distraction: the thief of focus, the thief of purpose, and the thief of time.

I put my life into three categories:

1. Urgent
2. Important
3. Fun

My urgent list is full of the most precious things to me: God, husband, kids, purpose and calling.

My important list is full of, well, important things to me or important things that have to get done: family, friends, church, volunteering, grocery shopping, doctor or dentist appointments, etc. These things have to get done for our lives to function, so they are essential.

My fun list is the best: vacations, spending time with friends, going for walks, playing board games, going to the beach, DISNEY WORLD (I would love for this to be on my urgent list), and taking a bath.

I prioritize my life so my life won't take priority!

My life is full, fun, busy, crazy, hectic, and can be all-consuming. However, I can't let it control me. I have to take control of my life and choose what is important based on my values and beliefs, based on what is important to me, and most importantly, what is important to God. Your life is a gift from God—every minute, day, year, and decade is precious. He filled it with every good thing you have. But when your good things become your only things and God becomes an unwelcome distraction in your life, then the life you were blessed with stops being blessed, and you become a slave to it.

Silenced by a life distracted away from God.

It is so easy to let life distract us, because we can see the need for us in it. I am needed by my husband and kids, I am needed at work, I am needed by my family, and I am needed by my friends. We put our worth in the things that distract instead of things that last, because we think that the things that are distracting us need us. We delegate doing the things that last to someone else—someone more qualified, more important, or experienced. As long as it's someone else, anyone else. You are needed by God; you and your purpose are needed in this battle.

In 1 Samuel, we read about the first king of Israel named Saul. He didn't start out as king, but he was hand-picked by God to become king. The prophet Samuel told Saul about the decision God made, but from the very beginning, Saul wasn't convinced. Saul didn't think he was good enough. He didn't trust God's plan, and he was distracted by insecurity.

"'. . . I am here to tell you that you and your family
are the focus of all Israel's hopes.'
Saul replied, 'But I'm only from the tribe of Benjamin,
the smallest tribe in Israel,
and my family is the least important of all the families
of that tribe!
Why are you talking like this to me?'"

1 SAMUEL 9:20b-21 NLT

Saul, the appointed king of Israel, never got past his feeling of unworthiness. He never grasped the importance of his purpose, and because of that, he never took it seriously. He never understood that the thoughts he had about himself were a distraction from his calling. He lived his life making up his own rules, following God's instructions halfheartedly, and trying to please others. He allowed himself to be distracted, because he didn't know just how important he was to God.

"And Samuel told him,
'Although you may think little of yourself,
are you not the leader of the tribes of Israel?
The LORD has anointed you king of Israel.

And the LORD sent you on a mission…'"

1 SAMUEL 15:17-18a NLT

"Although you may think little of yourself." Samuel called out Saul's insecurity and his distraction, and then followed up with a question: "Are you not the leader of the tribes of Israel?" I don't believe Samuel was looking for an answer; he was leading Saul to the answer and reminding him of his calling and purpose. Samuel goes on to say, "The Lord has anointed you... the Lord sent you on a mission."

We are anointed and appointed to change the world for Jesus. We have been sent on a mission and have been commissioned and positioned to live out the purpose God has infused inside each of us. Distraction, feelings of unworthiness, or being unqualified are no excuse for disobedience.

Christian women of this world–God's army–although you may think little of yourselves, have you not been anointed and appointed to change the world for Jesus?

When we don't know how important our purpose is and how critical it is to live it out, we allow ourselves to be distracted, we allow ourselves to be silenced, and we allow distraction to bring us down to a bow. We were created on purpose and with a purpose. We were created to change the world for Jesus. This must be on our urgent list. This must be a priority. This must be our mission. This is not sacrificing, even though sometimes it will feel like it, this is a privilege. It is a privilege to be chosen by God to change the world for him, and it is an honor to tell his story.

Saul thought he was sacrificing everything by becoming king. He thought he was doing the right thing, and felt his plans were right because they were right to him. His intentions were good, but his intentions were not God's plans or commands. Saul wanted to please God with his sacrifice, but God never asked him for that. He asked him for obedience and submission.

"But Samuel replied,

'What is more pleasing to the LORD:

your burnt offerings and sacrifices
or your obedience to his voice?
Listen! Obedience is better than sacrifice
and submission is better than offering...'"
1 SAMUEL 15:22a NLT

When God wants you to sacrifice, he will tell you. Until then, he wants your obedience, he wants your submission, and he wants to be first on your urgent list.

Your purpose is way too important to be distracted by everyday life. You were created to change the world, not to be changed by your world.

In chapter one, I told you my story about distraction. James was purposed to be in full-time ministry, but I didn't want him to serve in that role. All my attention and focus were on his place of employment rather than his purpose. If I'm being completely honest with myself and you, I didn't truly care about his purpose or the impact he would make; I was more concerned about the impact it would have on my life. I truly believed that agreeing with James to go into full-time ministry and be employed by a church was a sacrifice, but I would tell myself it was for the greater good, for James' happiness, and for God. In reality, I wasn't sacrificing anything, and I was dishonoring God.

I willingly bowed down to distraction. If God was trying to speak to me, I didn't hear it; if he was trying to guide me, I never saw it; and if he was trying to correct me, I never realized it. The enemy had me right where he wanted me—silenced by distraction.

One summer after James starting working at the church, the kids and I took a trip with my parents to see my brother, who lived in a different state. While we were there, we attended church. I don't remember the church's name or the pastor's name, but I do remember the story he told.

One evening, he and his wife were sitting in the living room together. He was reading, and she was sewing a set of curtains for her clients—she was an interior designer and loved her work. She was about three-quarters of the way finished with the curtains when she realized she had made a mistake, so she carefully started taking the seams out one at a time, by hand. The pastor said he began to feel frustrated for her while she sat there calmly fixing her mistake. God spoke to him at that moment and said, "Don't get frustrated for her, she is using the gifts and talents I gave her. You are watching her live out her purpose."

God used that story to speak to me, and at that moment, I knew I had been selfish. All this time, I wasn't just distracted, I was *distracting.* James was living out his purpose in front of my eyes, but I couldn't see it. James had pushed past my attempt at distracting him and was obedient to God, in spite of my best efforts to stop him.

If James had given into my distraction, he would have missed out on the last 17 years of full-time service to God. He would have missed out on stepping into his purpose. The thousands and thousands of people who have been impacted by his obedience would have missed out. When I look back, I am ashamed of my actions and repentant for my disobedience and my attempts at distracting James from his purpose.

From then on, I have never missed an opportunity to watch James live out his purpose.

To change the world for Jesus, we have to be neither distracted nor distracting. We can't discourage each other or step in each other's way. We have to be unified in one thing–obedience to God. If we are united in this one thing, we will not distract each other–instead we will inspire, encourage, motivate, and spur each other on.

"Two people are better off than one, for they can help each other succeed."

ECCLESIASTES 4:9 NLT

I am inspired daily by James and many other people who are focused on their mission of being obedient to God and not distracted by their lives or this world. They know who they are in Christ. They know they were created on purpose—they know what their purpose is, and they will not be distracted from it. The solution to distraction is Jesus. If we keep our eyes on him, keep our ears tuned to his voice, and stay focused on the purpose he put inside of each of us, we will be less likely to be fooled by distraction.

Daily time spent in conversation with him will keep us focused on what is urgent. Daily time spent getting to know his character and his love for us through reading the Bible will show us what is important. Being obedient to what he has purposed us to do will be fun—not just fun—but a blast and the ride of a lifetime. I know from experience that you will never regret choosing obedience over distraction. Never! Look straight ahead, and fix your eyes on what lies before you.

"Mark out a straight path for your feet;
stay on the safe path; Don't get sidetracked;
keep your feet from following evil."
PROVERBS 4:26-27 NLT

Jesus is the hope of the world, and we are his messengers. We deliver the good news of Jesus, tell of forgiveness and hope, and model freedom in Christ. We cannot be distracted; we have to be focused on finding every possible way to share Jesus. We have to make the best use of our time, and we have to believe that God has chosen us and appointed us to change the world for him.

"Some men came carrying a paralyzed man on a sleeping mat. They tried to take him inside to Jesus, but they couldn't reach him because of the crowd. So, they went up to the roof and took off some tiles. Then they lowered the sick man on his mat down into the crowd, right in front of Jesus. Seeing their faith, Jesus said to

the man, 'Young man, your sins are forgiven...' 'Stand up, pick up your mat, and go home!'"

LUKE 5:18-20,24b NLT

The men carrying the paralyzed man were not distracted from their goal of getting their friend to Jesus. When their path was blocked, they climbed up to the roof. If there was a problem, they were going to find a solution. Can you imagine how hard that was? I struggle to get on the roof carrying only my own weight and using a ladder. They were carrying a paralyzed man who couldn't help them at all. But that didn't stop them; they were focused on their mission.

After what I am sure was an exhausting trek to the top of the house, they then had to pull up roof tiles and roofing, make a hole big enough for a man to fit through, and make a way to Jesus. They had to be determined, focused, and free of distractions.

They are so close! The men can see Jesus through the hole, now all they have to do is get their friend down to the feet of Jesus. The Bible doesn't say how, but I'm sure it was just as creative as the way they got him up on the roof and then dug through the roof. When you are focused, creativity has room to bloom, and these men were focused. Their friend's healing depended on it.

The paralyzed man was now at the feet of Jesus.

The young man would never have made it to the feet of Jesus, and he never would have been forgiven of his sins and healed if it wasn't for "some men" who were focused, determined, creative, and cared enough about this man to put his life on their urgent list.

This is a beautiful example of love for the lost and those in need of healing. They modeled how focused we should be in bringing people to Jesus—no distraction, no distracting, just pure faith in Jesus and love for everyone he loves.

My favorite part of the story are these three words, "seeing their faith." He wasn't just talking about the paralyzed young man. He was talking to all of them. Jesus saw the faith of the men who wouldn't be stopped until their friend was healed, and he was moved. Their faith motivated them to act on behalf of a man who couldn't do it for himself. Jesus saw himself in those men; he saw his love shining through them, and he saw men who knew the difference one encounter with Jesus can make.

You are purposed to bring people to the feet of Jesus, especially people who can't make it there on their own. They need your faith, your determination, and your do- whatever-it-takes attitude. The battle needs you!

We, the Christian women of the world, choose to silence distraction and embrace the purpose and calling God has given us. We choose to see our calling not as a sacrifice but as obedience and submission. We choose to bring people to Jesus and not be discouraged or distracted, but courageous and focused. We must find a way, even when it looks like there is no way, to bring people to the feet of Jesus. We choose to change the world for Jesus.

When you choose no longer be silenced by distraction, but instead choose to stand in the face of it, you are not alone. God is standing right beside you. He stands next to you and says, "Now this is a girl I can change the world through."

11 THE ARMY

We, the women of the world– half of God's army–SILENCED NO LONGER.

We are not victims of this sinful world but rather volunteers to change it. We are volunteers in the army of Christ.

We were created resilient, strong, caring, compassionate, loving, hopeful, courageous, skilled, intelligent, creative, and passionate, to name a few.

We are risk takers, heart menders, advice givers, faith builders, world changers, and history makers.

Not one of us are all these things, but each of us is some of these things, and together we are an army. We are a volunteer army. We are women created by God on purpose and for a purpose. We were created to change the world around us for Jesus.

We are women no longer silenced by fear, pain, doubt, unforgiveness, shame, offense, pride, culture, and distraction. Half of God's army standing up, bravely joining the fight– aware that the battle being fought requires all of us to make a stand using our purpose, calling, actions, and voice to bring Jesus into our world again.

We live in a time where women are no longer afraid to stand up for our beliefs and fight for the right to choose the life God has laid out for us.

Women are making progress. We are changing the world. We are making a difference.

Women of God who are no longer afraid or ashamed to stand up to culture, no longer ashamed or afraid to stand up for Jesus, share Jesus, follow Jesus as he leads us, step into our purpose and calling, and encourage each other to live their purpose. We are no longer focused on ourselves, but on a lost and broken world. A world that needs Jesus! A world that needs your God-given purpose. No longer silent, but ready and willing to share Jesus with everyone we cross paths with: the lost, strayed, injured, weak, broken, enslaved, forgotten, abused, neglected, unseen, unheard and defenseless.

Years ago, while driving home on a dark stretch of highway late one winter night, I woke up to the need to share Jesus with everyone and anyone and at any given time.

I was driving along, enjoying the freeway without traffic. There was just one other SUV on the road, and I watched as they quickly sped past me. I am a bit competitive, so I contemplated speeding up to pass them, but I had precious cargo—my 4-year-old son Kyle and 1-year-old daughter Nichelle were safely and happily strapped in their car seats in the backseat. I wanted to keep it that way, so the need to compete quickly dissolved.

Mere seconds later, that same SUV quickly changed lanes, swerved back again to their lane, and then sharply crossed two lanes; it was evident that the driver had lost control of the vehicle. I watched as it hit the median wall, then flip across all four lanes over and over, until it landed upside down on the side of the highway.

Without thinking, I pulled over to the side of the road, only feet from the overturned SUV. I turned my hazards on, locked the doors, and ran to the upside-down vehicle. As I was running to the SUV, my mind began flashing pictures of what I might see when I got there, and for a split second, I wanted to run back to the safety of my car. As I arrived at the crushed vehicle, four men and a young girl, who had to be around 14-years-old, were climbing out of the broken windows. Instinctively, I ran to the young girl who was severely shaken, crying, and bleeding, wearing only jeans and a short sleeve shirt. It was freezing that night, so I quickly took my jacket off and wrapped her in it, then held her in my arms as she shook and cried uncontrollably.

By the grace of God, this girl was alive, and by the grace of God, I was there with her. I knew what I had to do; I watched as this young girl had a brush with death, and my immediate thought was, *If she had died in that accident her eternity would have been sealed.* That knowledge shook me to my core and propelled me to action. I had to share Jesus with her; I had to make sure that I did not let her walk away without knowing who saved her life that night. Without giving myself time to talk myself out of it, I said, "You are still alive for a reason: Jesus loves you, and he protected you." She responded, "I haven't been to church since I was a little girl," as if that disqualified her from being cared about by Jesus.

Right there on the side of the dark highway, in the freezing cold while sirens were blaring as the first responders were racing to get to us, I told her about Jesus. I reinforced the stories about Jesus she heard as a little girl, and then the most precious moment came when she prayed to accept Jesus into her life. A few minutes later, with my jacket still wrapped around her, she was loaded into an ambulance and whisked away. I never got her name, and I never saw her again; but Jesus knows her name, and he was and still is with her.

I silently walked back to my car, got in, and drove home. I tucked my little ones in bed, prayed over them, went downstairs and sobbed. I thanked God for allowing me to be there for the young girl, and I thanked him for the opportunity to tell her about Jesus and for the privilege of praying with her. As I was praying, doubt started to set in. What if she was in shock and doesn't remember, or what if she was in a desperate place and would have prayed anything, what if, what if. ... Then God spoke ever so gently to my sensitive heart. He said, "You did your job. You were there, and you shared Jesus with her. You prayed with her, now the rest is up to me." With that, I felt peace!

We, the Christian women of the world, are willing to pull over, stop in our tracks, make time for the lost, and run to the hurting. We vow to take every opportunity to share Jesus with a world on the edge of death. With eyes wide open, we look for people who need Jesus. We will be the generation that speaks up and stands up for a world that is out of control and on the brink of destruction. We have an internal alarm that God has put in our hearts: The alarm is sounding and beeping to the beat of eternity. For too long we have silenced this alarm–for too long we have ignored it. Now is the time, we feel its urgency humming in us and around us. We are waking up; we are standing up and fulfilling our purpose and calling for this time and for this generation.

"Yet God has made everything beautiful for its own time.
He has planted eternity in the human heart,
but even so, people cannot see the whole scope of God's work from beginning to end."
ECCLESIASTES 3:11 NLT

Our mission isn't to save anyone: it is to introduce them to the One who will.
Our mission isn't to convince anyone: it is to introduce them to the Truth.
Our mission isn't to heal anyone: it is to bring them to the Healer.
Our mission isn't to fight with anyone: it is to fight for them.

We are messengers in his army, sharing the message of Jesus, speaking the truth in love, and letting God do the rest. Our heart breaks for what his heart breaks for, as we search just as he does for the lost, strayed, injured, and weak. We vow to share Jesus with them the way Jesus has shown himself to us.

"I will search for the lost and bring back the strays.
I will bind up the injured and strengthen the weak."
EZEKIEL 34:16a NIV

Jesus searches for the lost, strayed, injured, and weak and brings them to us or brings us to them. Silent no more, we use our voice to bring healing, hope, salvation, restoration and... JESUS. Day and night, generation after generation, he seeks out his lost kids, willing and wanting to make them whole. Day and night, generation after generation, he is raising his army to go out into all the world and share the good news of Jesus. Generation after generation, he searches the world for the willing and ready, for his army. He has found the willing generation, right now–**it is us**!

We are making progress. We are changing the world. We are making a difference.

We now have the right to stand up for the unborn. We have the right to introduce women to Jesus' grace and forgiveness. We are obligated to share with women around the world that they are not alone. They have a choice, and they and their unborn baby matter to God. They were created on purpose and with a purpose.

We are making progress. We are changing the world. We are making a difference.

We have the right and mandate to speak up in every school around the world about our relationship with Jesus and our Christian beliefs. We have to pray and share the hope and healing we have found in Jesus with a generation that is killing themselves over bullying, depression, loneliness, anxiety, and rejection. We get to teach our kids to stand up for Jesus—to not be afraid or ashamed but to stand up and silence fear, doubt, and pressure.

We are making progress. We are changing the world. We are making a difference.

We now have the right to share the truth about love. The truth that no relationship will ever be fulfilling unless Jesus is in it. We can't marry whomever we want or be whatever gender we want to be; we don't get to throw God's workmanship and masterpiece out the window and believe that we know better than him. We have the right to speak the truth—God's truth—without judgment or shame.

We have the right and mandate to stand up for the abused, trafficked, sold, forgotten, unseen, unheard, persecuted, and discarded by the world. Women, the Army of God, standing up for our sisters, arms linked around the world, encircling the vulnerable and sharing the Healer of all wounds with them.

The world will tell us. You are making progress. You are changing the world. You are making a difference. The world will be right!

We shape the world with the sound of our voice. We cast our vote when we speak up, and we stand up by taking action. No longer silent, we are changing the world, and we are making a difference.

We boldly take these steps, and so many others, because we know why we do it, we know who we are doing it for, and we are confident in the difference one encounter with Jesus can make.

Jesus: the first volunteer, the first to make a stand, and the first to change our world.

Jesus stood on the cross, arms outstretched, welcoming our sin, fear, doubt, unforgiveness, shame, brokenness, rebellion, and silence. On that cross, he stood up for us, he stood up with us, and he stood up to our accusers. He did it without hesitation, and he did it with love and compassion for us, knowing that his sacrifice would render us free. We are free from an eternity in Hell, free from the bondage of culture, free from shame, free from pain, and free to change the world for him, using the purpose and calling that he created us with.

"...Because of the joy awaiting him, he endured the cross,
disregarding its shame.
Now he is seated in the place of honor beside God's throne."
HEBREWS 12:2b NLT

If Jesus didn't feel shame, neither should we! Neither should we!

We will not be ashamed. We will not be silent, because we know that the next generation is watching and waiting to see what legacy we will leave for them. We will not be ashamed, because we know people need Jesus and culture needs to be changed. Fear, pain, doubt, unforgiveness, shame, offense, pride, culture, and distraction need to be brought to a bow before Jesus.

Today, we are dealing with the consequences of the silent generations before us. We were handed a world that is used to taking the voice God gave them and using it against him. We are used to hearing wrong called right, used to being shamed for our beliefs, used to compromising our faith, and used to being silent. Silenced with marches, chants, and bobbing signs, we were intimidated; we accepted defeat, and we silently bowed.

NO LONGER!

We are the generation who will no longer be silenced, and we will not pass a silenced voice to the next generation. We will not be fearful, doubtful, unforgiving, shamed, offended, prideful, distracted, or bullied by culture.

NO, we will be a beacon of hope, a light in the darkness, the voice of truth, the helping hand and crying shoulder, the uncompromised in our faith, the courageous in the sharing of Jesus, the prayer warrior, the Bible reader, the church attender, the generous giver, the leader, teacher and preacher, and the ones who stand when the rest of the world bows.

"You are the light of the world—like a city on a hilltop that cannot be hidden."

MATTHEW 5:14 NLT

We are making progress. We are changing the world. We are making a difference.

My kids and I were sitting in the church office after a Sunday service waiting on James, who was in a meeting. We were talking about what we should eat for lunch, when a lady, who I recognized as a greeter, and a gentleman walked in and asked, "Has anyone turned in a Bible?" I was about to help them look for it when the gentleman said with relief in his voice, "Here it is." The matter seemed settled, so we went back to talking about lunch. Then I heard the greeter ask, "Do you have proof that this Bible belongs to you? Is your name written anywhere in it?" My kids and I looked at each other with a smile. This greeter took her job seriously, and no one was going to take home a Bible that didn't belong to them on her watch.

He unzipped the brown leather Bible cover and started flipping through the pages trying to find something that proved this Bible belonged to him. He stopped and pulled out a bookmarker with the word Grace written across it in big bold letters. He said, "I don't have anything with my name on it." He showed her the bookmarker and said, "This was my wife's Bible. Her name was Grace–she passed away."

I wasn't privileged to know Grace or her story, but her life impacted me. She lived a life devoted to getting to know her Savior, a life cherishing God's Word. When she passed away, her husband knew in order to stay close to her, he needed to keep her most prized possession close to him, so he replaced his Bible with hers. She was created on purpose and with a purpose. She was created to change the world for Jesus, and even though she is no longer on this earth, her commitment to Jesus is still changing the world. Her life impacted me, and through me, this generation, and through this generation, it will impact the next generation.

We are an army united by God himself. We are an army with the common goal of sharing Jesus with the world. We are an army who wants the next generation to carry the message of Jesus forward. We are an army who wants to stop and drown out the voice of the enemy with the message and righteousness of Jesus.

We will make a difference; God is counting on us. He's calling us to unite, to link arms in our Christ-centered beliefs, to defeat and overwhelm the enemy's message with the message of Jesus, and to stand with confidence and courage. He is calling us to speak as one voice and march as one army.

Today is the day you start, and today is the day you look for opportunities to share Jesus with your world: your husband, your kids, your family, your friends, your neighbors, your co-workers, and anyone who will listen.

It was the last week of our Bible study. My small group decided to meet at a local fast food restaurant for a change of scenery. We had just finished our study, when one of the cashiers strategically made her way to us while mopping. She asked what we were doing. We told her we were doing a Bible study about the power of words and what Jesus has to say about us and to us.

She looked at the books on the table and said, "I've been looking for something like that to read." Without hesitation, my friend Karen gave the young lady her book. She didn't tell her where to find the book or wait and look to the rest of us for a solution. She acted and immediately gave the cashier her book. The young lady was so grateful and excited, she grabbed the book, leaving the mop behind. As we were leaving, we tried to wave goodbye to her, but she was way too busy reading the book she was just given to notice us.

Today is the day you start! There is no wrong time to share Jesus with the people around you, and there is no gesture too small, no circumstance too big. Eternity hangs in the balance. Now is the time! Now is the time to stand!

Go into the world ready to share the good news with everyone!

"And then he told them,
'Go into all the world and preach the Good News to everyone.
Anyone who believes and is baptized will be saved.
But anyone who refuses to believe will be condemned.'"

MARK 16:15-16 NLT

"Therefore, go and make disciples of all the nations,
baptizing them in the name of the Father and the Son and the Holy Spirit.
Teach these new disciples to obey all the commands I have given you.
And be sure of this:
I am with you always, even to the end of the age."

MATTHEW 28:19-20 NLT

"And be sure of this: I am with you always, even to the end of the age."

We are God's army; we fight for and with him, and we are accompanied and led by him.

And you can be sure of this: He is with us until our end and the end. He is the creator and the finisher of all things both on earth and in Heaven. He is the creator and finisher of all purpose in you and lived through you, even to the end.

When you choose to no longer be silenced, but instead choose to stand, you are not alone. God is standing right beside you. He stands next to you and says,

"Now this is a girl I can change the world through!"

Women: the army of God. Created on purpose and with a purpose. Created to change the world around us for Jesus.

THE MAKINGS OF THE SILENCED ARMY

The day I sat down to write this book was a day like any other. I didn't plan to write this book; I didn't even know this book was inside of me, waiting for the God-ordained time to come out.

My husband, James, and I were talking about women in the big "C" church–women who are persecuted for their belief in and devotion to Christ. And we were talking about the women in America who want to *be* more, *do* more, *start* more, *lead* more and *preach* more for the causes of Christ.

I flippantly said, "One day I am going to write a book titled, *The Silent Army*." I quickly followed that thought process as chapter titles began taking shape in my mind. I could hear James talking to me in the far distance, but a book was being born in that moment, and I didn't hear a word he said. Then, it hit me; this book would be titled: *The Silenced Army.*

The title reflected how my life had been for too many years. Silenced by fear, pain, doubt, unforgiveness, shame, offense, pride, culture and distraction. I was part of God's army, and I had chosen silence; I chose to bow. Instantly, in my mind, I saw millions of ladies just like me who have been hurt, abused, shamed and silenced, I saw an army of women who could change the world for Jesus but instead were choosing silence.

It became immediately clear to me that *The Silenced Army* had to be written. I shared this with James right away, to which he said, "Write your thoughts down, so when you are ready to write this book, you will have notes to reference." As soon as he left for work, I sat down to write my thoughts down, and by the time James got home from work, the first two chapters were written. I couldn't have stopped if I had wanted to. It was as if the words were flowing out of me like a rushing river. I was typing as fast as I could, but I was having trouble keeping up with my thoughts. And within seven days, the first draft of this book was completed.

I may have written this book in seven days, but it was in the making for forty-one years. God did not waste one experience, one heartache, one painful moment or one ounce of healing in my life. He purposed all of it to inspire, motivate and mobilize His daughters, His masterpieces, His army to change the world for Jesus.

It is a privilege and an honor to steward and share this message that God has written on my heart, and I would love to be a part of your next event or conference. One of my favorite lines in this book is; *"He only has to silence one of us to silence the rest, for if one of us speaks up, it gives courage to the rest."*

To learn more about Nichole or to book her for your next event or conference, visit nicholechavez.com or email her at info@nicholechavez.com.

NEW STUDY TO CONTINUE THE JOURNEY

If you've enjoyed this book, now you can go deeper with the companion Study Guide!

In this ten-week book study that corresponds with *The Silenced Army*, you are given the tools to silence fear, pain, doubt, unforgiveness, shame, offense, pride, culture, and distraction. I don't like to cook, but I do cook at least five dinners a week because I've been told my family requires food to survive. One of the tools I have found that makes my dreaded nightly cooking session easier is this genius thing called a meal kit. All I have to do is choose how many meals I want per week, and how many I'm making dinner for, and they will send me everything I need. In fact, they have everything measured out and cut up for me—and on top of that—they send step-by-step instructions so I know exactly how to put everything together to get the desired outcome of a tasty meal. Now I don't dread it so much, and my family can enjoy more than my three go-to meals week after week.

This study is a little like a meal kit. I have researched the Scriptures, I've given you the instructions, and I've measured out your daily study time, but the rest is up to you. You have to put the ingredients together, you have to follow the step-by-step instructions, and you have to apply it to get the desired results - the God results.

Available now at nicholechavez.com.

NEW DEVOTIONAL STUDY FOR YOUR SMALL GROUP

Discover God's unique, world-changing purpose hidden inside of you!

What is your purpose? Have you ever stopped to think about how you fit into God's greater plan and what role He designed you to play? Have you had thoughts of purpose, but felt too insignificant or lost to embark on the journey of discovering your unique purpose? Do you long for purpose, but have no idea where to start?

Everyone's purpose is different—and so is the journey you must undergo to discover and fulfill it. You may have lived a life that is good, bad, hurtful, painful, happy, sad, devastating, but God weaves them together with threads of grace and forgiveness, healing and restoration. He takes your life as a whole and uses it for His purpose and your good.

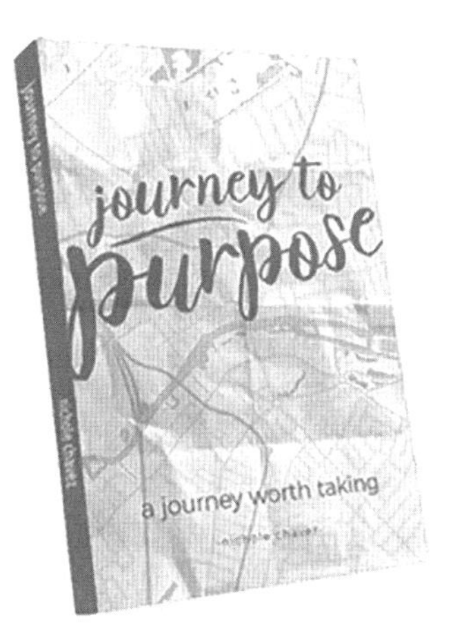

The journey requires perseverance and a commitment to personal honesty. In this six-week study, Nichole shows you how to:

Reveal your hidden purpose
Accept your unique purpose
Step into your extraordinary purpose . . .

Along the way, you'll learn valuable lessons from real people throughout the Bible that labored to find their purpose, you'll reflect on fresh insights, you'll pray for God's guidance and begin living out your newfound purpose.

This is your journey. Let's get started.

Available now at nicholechavez.com.

NICHOLECHAVEZ.COM

We live in unique times of women empowerment, influence, leadership, and strength, but having these incredible privileges is not what matters; how we use them is what matters most. I believe women can change the world; I believe we can change the world for Jesus. God has a plan for your voice, your life, your freedom, your influence, your leadership, and your strength, He wants to take the incredible gifts we have and use them to bring a hurting and broken world to Him.

Nichole Chavez Ministries exists for this sole purpose: "To build a community of women from around the world to change the world for Jesus. To no longer look at ourselves as victims of a sinful world but as volunteers to change it."

- Nichole

Join this community of women who are excited about changing the world for Jesus.

nicholechavez.com